RHONDA ANDERSON

THE WORKPLACE

To every thing there is a season

Copyright © 2018 Rhonda Anderson

All rights reserved. No part of this book may be used or reproduced by any means, graphic, electronic, or mechanical, including photocopying, recording, taping or by any information storage retrieval system without the written permission of the publisher except in the case of brief quotations embodied in critical articles and reviews.

Unless indicated, Scripture quotations are taken from the King JamesVersion of the Bible.
Scriptures taken from the Holy Bible, New International Version®, NIV®. Copyright © 1973, 1978, 1984, 2011 by Biblica, Inc.™ Used by permission of Zondervan. All rights reserved worldwide. www.zondervan.com The "NIV" and "New International Version" are trademarks registered in the United States Patent and Trademark Office by Biblica, Inc.™ All rights reserved.

Word definitions by Merriam-Webster, Merriam-Webster's Collegiate Dictionary, Eleventh Edition, principal copyright 2003, and https://www.merriam-webster.com
Because of the vigorous nature of the Internet, any web addresses or links contained in this book may have changed since publication and may no longer be valid.

Word definitions indicated by The Prophets Dictionary, Paula Price, The Prophet's Dictionary, Revised and Expanded Edition (New Kensington, PA: Whitaker House, 2006).

Book cover design: Front cover image by Angel Impressions; Back cover image by Alpha Image Photography. All rights reserve.

Pillar Publishing & Company, LLC.
Richmond, VA
www.pillarpublishingcompany.org
info@pillarpublishingcompany.org

The publisher is not responsible for websites or content that are not owned by the publisher.

Book Edited by: [1] Book Help Online Services; [2] Pillar Publishing & Company Editorial Service

ISBN: 978-0-9983417-0-5 (print)
ISBN: 978-0-9983417-1-2 (eBook)

Library of Congress Control Number: 2018942271

Contents

CHAPTER 1 15
   THE WORKPLACE INTRODUCTION 15

CHAPTER 2 21
   THE MESSAGE 21

CHAPTER 3 33
   WRESTLING WITH PURPOSE 33

CHAPTER 4 53
   SEASONS TELL TIME 53

CHAPTER 5 207
   PRAYERS FOR THE WORKPLACE 207
      Thanking God for Our Workplace 207
      Prayer for Our Leaders in the Workplace 209
      Prayer for Wrestling with Our Purpose 211
      Prayer to Help Us Through Our Seasons 213
      Praying for One Another in the Workplace 215

NOTES 217

To every thing there is a season, and a time to every purpose under the heaven.
(Ecclesiastes 3:1–8)

CHAPTER 1

THE WORKPLACE INTRODUCTION

CHAPTER 1

THE WORKPLACE INTRODUCTION

Your entire life has a place on earth that is very significant to our Father in heaven. We all have a workplace in God's divine plan. This message is a mind-set change for some and increased knowledge for others—mainly expanding our understanding of how special we really are. The intent of this book is to take you deeper into the mysteries of God and how your life was strategically mapped out before you were even born. For God to know the beginning of your life, and the ending, therefore everything in between is also known to Him.

We live in a time when it is vital that we understand more about our purpose. Having gone through several life-changing experiences pertaining to the workplace, I was led to seek out why we endure immeasurable encounters and different experiences in the working environment. I knew there had to be a larger picture than what I was seeing. I have learned that all my answers are in the Word of God; He speaks to us through His Word. This journey has blessed me beyond measure.

Everyone is a laborer in God's view and has a workplace assignment on earth. Wherever your workplace is, it has a direct impact to your everyday life. This impact is not limited to a job as we know it, or to working hours, as we are still living life even when sleeping. Life and time do not wait because we are asleep. As laborers, everything we do is accounted for.

Our natural workplace is only a moving peg on the map of life that God uses. One of the strongest points to truly understand is that there is a greater purpose than just a paycheck. The paycheck is only one resource designed for us to use in our purpose-driven lives. God never intended for us to be bound by a paycheck. The paycheck is tangible and has been treated as a personal treasure, but it is a lie created by the enemy to keep us conforming to worldly thinking as opposed to seeing the true purpose of pay for wages. A paycheck serves a purpose, but it is not "the purpose" for your life. Because the workplace is a part of our purpose, we will experience many challenges that impact the fulfillment of our purpose. For that reason, and as the foundational driver behind this book, prayer is crucial for the working environment, because it is tied to your purpose.

Wherever purpose is, prayer should be also. I have found that without prayer we limit our access to more understanding. Prayer is the infrastructure that builds our relationship with our Father in heaven. When you pray it opens the communication between you and God. Our prayers are personal, and the intent is relationship based. As prayer builds the relationship with God, we obtain a greater understanding of our true purpose here on earth.

Everyone may not pray as they ought to, but at some point, we will all realize how much we need God, and prayer is the entry point. It does not matter how many words you use in the conversation, but it does start with words. What do you have to lose? Just start talking to Him and each time the conversation will increase, as will your relationship with God. No one knows you like God does. He created you.

In addition, it is good to pray with others and it is also sometimes necessary for intercession, especially in the workplace. However, we must remember that each one of us has our own unique path in life and we will meet God face-to-face one day. My opinion is, it is better to know Him before that day. Therefore, everyone should embrace having a prayer life.

This book was written from a biblical perspective because I believe anything that impacts our life should have a spiritual foundation. The preferred references are used because the Bible is not only one of the oldest books, but it also contains infallible wisdom pertaining to life. Furthermore, as a believer and follower of Jesus Christ, I strongly hold fast to the proven fact that he is our example for life. More significantly, to realize that even Jesus was a laborer and had workplaces during his life here on earth. This book has a Mission and a Message to the world with an overarching kingdom Goal:

- The Mission of this book is to enlighten the reader (laborer), from a spiritual perspective, in areas concerning the workplace. The book conjointly brings forth a common view as to why we face so many challenges in our workplace and how they are tied to our individual purpose. The view will also bring to light why it is important to pray without ceasing concerning our workplace.

- The Inspired Message is to reveal God's greater purpose of our work assignments while we are here on the earth. The book will address themes pertaining to the "workplace" and "laborers" to help with us understand the workplace purpose and process.

- The book's Goal is to continue to spread the gospel of the kingdom to all nations and to carry on the edification to the body of Christ.

The book also includes some written prayers to help intercede in the following areas:

1. Leaders in the workplace
2. Wrestling with purpose
3. Seasons within the workplace
4. Praying for one another in the workplace

CHAPTER 2

THE MESSAGE

CHAPTER 2

THE MESSAGE

For by Him all things were created that are in heaven and that are on earth, visible and invisible, whether thrones or dominions or principalities or powers. All things were created through Him and for Him. (Colossians 1:16)

The workplace can be identified as any physical place where there is an assignment with a purpose, driven by a process. The message of this book speaks to all laborers. The list below gives several types, but is not limited to what is itemized:

- Corporate workers
- Fast-food workers
- Construction workers
- Ministry or church workers
- Small business workers
- Student or educational workers
- Housewives
- Mentors
- Teachers
- Domestic or janitorial workers
- Army, Navy, Marines, Air Force workers
- Musicians
- Caregivers
- Coaches

- Hospitality workers
- Government officials
- Transportation drivers
- Retired workers
- Untitled workers
- Every person on this earth to whom God has given life to be a laborer with a workplace.

Satan also has laborers working for him; they are just working for the wrong team. Work is always a continuing process. Work was designed or created by God who is the Creator of everything. As long as the earth remains, there will always be a workplace and laborers. Each laborer's time will end, but the work will go on until the end of time.

Our jobs are instrumental in God's purpose and plan for our lives. Understanding the divine assignment of a job and how it can impact our spiritual growth and relationship with God gives us another perspective on life. Your job is a vital key to your purpose here on earth. Whenever something impacts purpose, there is a great need for prayer, and even more so, there is a higher demand to intercede for individuals we work with.

WORK DRIVEN BY PROCESS

Since the beginning of time, work has existed. Work has always had a purpose, and that purpose is driven by a process. Now, the process can change, but the purpose will stay the same. In most cases, process change comes about in the name of improvement. When there is a change during the process, we as people are not always flexible enough to adhere to it. This is because we are naturally driven by flow and comfort zones, and anything that interrupts our flow can cause a distraction in how we view the purpose. God is the Creator of our purpose, and we must remember that His thoughts are not our thoughts, nor His ways the same as ours. This is why we should build a strong relationship with God to gain understanding.

> For my thoughts are not your thoughts, neither are your ways my ways, saith the Lord. (Isaiah 55:8)

It is so easy to lose sight of our purpose in life. God has a purpose for each one of us, and it is built into His master plan. From the time we were formed within the womb, a purpose has been attached to us. It is up to us to find our purpose on the earth.

In some workplaces, we find that there are specific tools to perform certain job functions. Those tools are used during the process of completing the work. I believe that we have some spiritual tools that can be used to get work done. These tools can aid us in finding our purpose.

SPIRITUAL TOOLS

- SPIRITUAL VISION

Our Spiritual Vison is revealed through the Holy Spirit that dwells within us. When you obtain this inward vision, you can view life from a spiritual perspective. The natural view becomes secondary.

- SPIRITUAL ROADMAP

The Roadmap is the Holy Scriptures (Bible). This roadmap (book) is comprised of work by various authors who were inspired to write the infallible Word of God. This map is a lamp or light upon our path in life. The scriptures offers the very history of life upon this earth in a written format. The Bible is available in many different translations, audio and visual products. This map offers any reader the wisdom and knowledge to face any situation concerning their purpose in life.

- SPIRIT OF LOVE

Lastly, love, which is the greatest gift of all (1 Corinthians 13). God is love, and because we are made in the very image of Him, so we possess the most powerful gift of all: love. When we truly understand our purpose, we will find that it is 100 percent wrapped in the purest of love.

UNIQUELY DESIGNED FOR WORK

God is the total source and visionary of life. When He created man, He purposed and fashioned him for work. Work is tied to the cycle of life. There are many different types of work components that can be tied to your purpose in life. In the second chapter from the book of Genesis, we see that Adam worked in the garden of Eden, which can be considered a workplace. The Word says in verse 2:8–9 that "the Lord God planted a garden…and out of the ground he made every tree grow," so this tells me that the Lord worked too. Common knowledge tells us that labor is involved in planting a garden, and how ever God performed the work, it was completed.

Adam's workplace was in the garden and there was a process in place that he was fulfilling. Wherever you have worked during your life, whether it was at home being a caretaker, a housewife, or at a physical work location, there was a system in place to be followed to complete the work.

We are all fashioned differently, and we function in diverse ways to fulfill the vision of life. Because God is the visionary of life, he operates on a much larger scale than we can see with our natural eyes. In some of our reasoning, we may not think that our daily work process ties in with God's greater plan, but it does. God never creates anything without a purpose. Every job has a purpose and is vital to a greater intent. We should never take our jobs for granted—your job has been handpicked by God and has a divine purpose.

WRESTLING CAN CAUSE A BOTTLENECK IN YOUR PURPOSE

Purpose is what holds everything together. Without purpose, there is no meaning, no value, and no vision. God does nothing without purpose. Fulfilling a purpose requires a plan, and every plan consists of a process. Wrestling with life processes can place a bottleneck in our purpose, meaning it can slow down the process of us completing our purpose. The message in the "Wrestling with Purpose" chapter will shed some light on what awaits us at the end of the process so long as we don't give up. Sometimes we do not realize how much we get in the way of what God is doing in our lives.

The workplace must be tied to our purpose as a laborer, else it would not exist. Some jobs we handpick through the "freewill" network choice. Therefore, the outcome or produced results can be somewhat different. Those choices can cause a delay in our purpose being manifested here on the earth.

SEASONS

There will always be changes in our lives. Distractions, interferences, obstacles, impediments come along to stop the work. When this happens, the process cannot continue. When the process comes to a halt, it causes a delay or shift in delivery. Every life has a delivery mark: we have a start date, and we have a delivery date.

- The start date is when we are born.

- The delivery date is referred to as our earthly expiration date.

These dates are attached to seasons, which are also considered as appointed times according to Ecclesiastes 3:1. Chapter 3 in this book takes a deep dive into seasons referenced in the Bible and how they can be mapped to the workplace. Dates can be significant, but seasons are more important because they do not contain dates. The process driven by purpose is what happens in between the start and delivery dates. Our work types can also be categorized as physical and spiritual. What we accomplish here on earth happens through both work categories. They both have a process through toil (work), and therefore, a purpose.

The physical work refers to our jobs that we have been given to toil with—the works of our hands. One thing we must never forget is that the enemy also knows our job is tied to our purpose. His goal is always to steal, kill and destroy anything that could cause us not to fulfill our divine purpose. Therefore, the enemy knows how to promote distractions. He understands God's concept for a purpose-driven life, and he wreaks havoc on our lives by using powers, principalities, spiritual wickedness, and other works of evil to prevent us from completing our process to accomplish our life's goal.

We know that Satan is a perpetrator of God, and his goal is the opposite of God's plan, so when we allow distractions to keep us in a wilderness state, it prolongs our blessing. Distractions come in many different forms. We need to have the wisdom to recognize the works of the enemy and use our map to get back on course. The race still has to be run, and the cycle of life has to continue.

> For we wrestle not against flesh and blood, but against principalities, against powers, against the rulers of the darkness of this world, against spiritual wickedness in high places. (Ephesians 6:12)

> The thief does not come except to steal, and to kill, and to destroy. I have come that they may have life, and that they may have it more abundantly. (John 10:10)

This book will take you through some life examples of the divine purpose of the workplace and you as the laborers. It will also show the connection to the mission and that the key to life is prayer. Prayer helps us endure the process; it builds us up and strengthens our inner man so that we are able to overcome in our areas of need.

As mentioned earlier, prayer functions as the very key and access to our heavenly Father. When we have access to the King of all kings, Lord of all lords, and Creator of heaven and earth, what other access could be greater? We are wealthy and don't even realize it. We are truly laborers unto God and the work we do on the earth, should be done unto Him.

You are the blessing in the workplace. How many times has God placed a blessing on your job just for you? If you were there breathing or operating in some capacity, then it was a blessing. Maybe you did not recognize that it was a blessing, or more importantly who the blessing was actually from. Nevertheless, you will read about some biblical and life cases to discover how the workplace can truly be a blessing beyond measure.

Lastly, another plug-in is how the workplace is a major part of your ministry. Some may feel that ministry is not for them, or some may say they do not have nor desire a ministry. But actually, ministry is for everyone, and we all have one whether we call it ministry or not. Ministry is work, and we all work in some form or fashion. Who we work for is also key to God's design for ministry.

CHAPTER 3

WRESTLING WITH PURPOSE

CHAPTER 3

WRESTLING WITH PURPOSE

As laborers, we must have a concise understanding of our purpose so that we will not struggle with life's process. Many of us will fight the process only to learn later that it was essential to our purpose. Everyone's workplace purpose is unique. My purpose in life differs from the next person's, and the workplace does as well. We can work for the same entity but have a different purpose for being there. God made us all exclusive individuals in His own reasoning, so everything that we do in life has a divine outcome.

In viewing the average work structure, a person spends about eight to ten hours a day in a working environment as we know it. For some, this time span consumes most of their waking hours, which tells us that our work time has a large impact on our life. Any area in our lives that consumes most of our functioning time is an indicator that can be tied back to God's plan for our life. I believe that we obtain two types of jobs: the one we choose out of free will, and the one that God has ordained for us. Both types need consistent prayer. I strongly believe that prayer should be a daily regimen, especially in the life of a believer in Jesus Christ. Although there are massive components that can make up a working environment, this chapter will focus on the purpose behind the workplace and laborers.

The first mention of the term work in the Bible is found in Genesis chapter 2, where it talks about how God rested from His creative works (labor) on the seventh day. The Hebrew word for work is mlakah (mel-aw-kaw)[1], meaning "occupation, business, and workmanship, as the result of labor." Work is ordained by God. We have been created in His image, and just as God works, we too have a mandate to work. In all of the creative works by God, there was and still is a divine purpose for labor on earth.

> And on the seventh day God ended his work which he had made; and he rested on the seventh day from all his work which he had made. And God blessed the seventh day, and sanctified it: because that in it he had rested from all his work which God created and made. (Genesis 2:2–3)

There are many areas of concern in the workplace that people face daily. There are many different types of working environments, but according to Ecclesiastes 1:9, there is no new thing under the sun. So, this tells me that all the different types of working environments have been experienced before. The process may have changed but the spiritual experience remains the same. This book may not cover each work type, but I refer you to the Holy Bible, which is a collection of books that holds a wealth of information concerning anything you need answers to.

> The thing that hath been, it is that which shall be; and that which is done is that which shall be done: and there is no new thing under the sun. (Ecclesiastes 1:9)

Over the course of my career I have held several different types of job. Many of them were not what I considered to be my ideal place to work, but with greater understanding I can identify that each job was tied to my purpose. Looking back at my work history, I recognize that my job was never about me, but about what God wanted to do within me. The amazing part about God's creative works is we can't always see Him knitting and weaving our lives together.

My first job I ever had was babysitting. I loved to hold and care for babies. My neighbors had small children and they would, on occasion, ask me to keep them. As I look back, I can see where the seed was being sown for my desire to love and nurture people. For me, my workplace foundation began in the home—a place where family and relationships are formed. Think about where your first work assignment was. It could be even a small task like cleaning up or mowing the grass. Nevertheless, that was the beginning of God grooming you for your purpose.

Your purpose had already been planned before you were even born. I believe God has shown me countless times how true His Word is. I have come to the realization that my life was already planned before I was formed in my mother's womb, according to Jeremiah 1:5. This was mentioned in the scriptures so that we would have knowledge of this. God foreknew his purpose as a prophet. He foreknew your purpose as well.

> Before I formed thee in the belly I knew thee; and before thou camest forth out of the womb I sanctified thee, and I ordained thee a prophet unto the nations. (Jeremiah 1:5)

I have been faced with many challenges in my life where certain choices would have taken me down a different road, but God's purpose for my life directed me on other paths. When the scriptures say that all things work together for the good for those who love God, and are called according to His purpose, it is true. There were times when I was mad because things did not go the way I wanted them to. Now I can see where there was a greater plan for my life. He has a great plan for you too. We may not see all of the details at times, but if you trust that he is God forever, you won't be disappointed at the end.

> And we know that all things work together for good to them that love God, to them who are the called according to his purpose. (Romans 8:28)

God is so much bigger than we give Him credit for. Our belief tends to sway at times because we see one thing in the natural, but we must remember that God is doing something else in the spiritual that will eventually result in the natural. Well, I believe this; you might as well trust Him because God does not change—He is the same yesterday, today and forever. God created you and gave you a purpose to live on this earth. Everything God creates is good, therefore you are good.

If God has you on a job, then it is tied to your destiny. Your destiny is the ultimate goal of what is already preordained. I mentioned in the introduction that the purpose of your job is beyond a paycheck, which is only a small benefit of having a job. God's purpose is universal. We may think we are working a job for one reason; but when God reveals your true purpose for your existence, you will view your job in a different light.

Now there are some jobs we choose that are not the will of God. An example could be illegal jobs or positions that promote lying, cheating, stealing, murdering, and other evil and wicked works. God created us with His likeness in mind; not of anything that would keep us separated from Him. So, if a person has a job that ties them to evil, then an immediate evaluation is necessary to determine who they are really working for. The lifeline of that job is short lived. We must remember that Satan is a counterfeiter, and he wants to deceive and destroy you at all costs. Your job was intended to be a blessing to you and to glorify God. If your works glorify Satan rather than God, you are off course; when you are not in alignment with God's purpose, it can change your destiny.

> For I know the thoughts that I think toward you, saith the Lord, thoughts of peace, and not of evil, to give you an expected end. (Jeremiah 29:11)

God never said that our work life would be easy. Even if your labor is in the home as a caretaker, stay at home parent, or retired from another work environment, there is still work to be done. As long as we live on the earth, God can still use you.

There will be times when our labor will seem as though there is no blessing in it due to the discomforts and pain we must endure. Our working pain is one of the main ingredients to the process of working toward purpose. There are people who are assigned to our purpose, and those people can sometimes inflict pain upon us. Pain never feels good, especially if they are growing pains.

I recall working my first corporate job. Being excited to work for a big company made me feel that I was growing toward what I thought my future would be. I started at an entry level in the mail room and worked my way "upstairs" to an administrative job, learning new things about the company and industry. In the mail room, everything was great and all the people I worked with seemed to be good people. However, when elevation happens in the physical world, it changes in the spiritual world as well. New levels bring new challenges, and if you are not prepared for them, they can cause pain. At first everything was fine, then management changed and there were new people. Before finishing the story, I want to highlight some things in here.

"New" marks a beginning of something, so we should pay close attention to what God is doing because most of the time it is the first indicator of a shift in the spiritual. Shift is good because if God does not shift, then things won't move. We always want to be moving toward our ultimate goal in life.

When you become a new person in the workplace or new people come into your life in the workplace, there is a purpose to it all. Not everyone will have the same input into your purpose, but they still have a purpose. This works both ways, meaning you can be tied to their purpose as well. There are three words to describe the purpose in the workplace. I call them the "3 Ps." They are reminders for the workplace, and they are all driven by process:

1. Prepare—you for the next workplace purpose (Ephesians 2:10)
2. Position—you to fulfill your purpose (Proverbs 16:3)
3. Push—you into the next level toward purpose (Jeremiah 29:11)

These are reminders that will help you focus on your purpose and be aware of other people's purposes as well. All three are process driven and can be painful at times. When purpose is turning the wheel of life, it can seem as though you are in this process alone and have been forgotten. We must remember that God will never leave us. Although it is hard to do at times, we must try not to complain when things are not going as we expect in the workplace, even when we assume that this process is not in our favor. Be encouraged by this scripture below:

Let your conversation be without covetousness; and be content with such things as ye have: for he hath said, I will never leave thee, nor forsake thee. (Hebrews 13:5)

The first point on the list is "prepare," because this should be at the top of your list. This is the most powerful key to your success story. To prepare something means that it is not ready yet. Merriam-Webster nicely describes prepare [2] as, "to make [someone or something] ready beforehand for some purpose, use, or activity." Preparation is purpose driven. When we are being prepared for something it has a purpose in mind. As long as we live, we are being prepared for what is to come. The preparation process endures until Christ returns. Our divine purpose is to prepare us to live forever. God has been preparing you for your purpose by using people ever since you were born. From your mother's womb to others that have interacted in your life.

In general, how well do we prepare for something? Most of the time we want to bypass the preparation process and move straight into the execution of something. That's not how God does it. He prepares you for success. Even the worst job has prepared you for greatness.

As mentioned earlier, the workplace can be anywhere God has assigned you. We have to be careful not to despise people who are in the workplace, even if they are a distraction. Some people have been placed in your life to help prepare you for your next assignment.

Picking back up where I left off about my first corporate job: before I had given my life to Christ, and understood spiritual things, when management changed, everything began to change. This new manager set goals that seemed unreachable and it seemed personal because she rode me so hard compared to some of the others. This went on for a while and I feared losing my job. It became so overwhelming and I wanted to stop feeling like I was in a war every day. Others appeared to be handling the new management okay but I was stressed out. One day, while feeling really heavy on the way to work, I decided to say a prayer. It wasn't any fancy words; I simply talked to God about my situation and how I was feeling. I did not have a deep relationship with God, but I knew to call on Him for help. Once I got into the building, I started running up the stairs for fear I would make the new manager angry if I arrived late.

I heard something say, "Stop running"; and I did.

I stood in the stairway for a little while, breathing hard, and I said, "I am tired."

At that moment, it was like something lifted off of me. When I got on the floor, she was waiting for me. I was immediately pulled into a room and I was released from that job. I was hurt, but I could not shed a tear.

I remember on the ride home saying to God, "Now what?" I could not hear any response, but there was a peace.

Peace is something that truly surpasses your understanding. My purpose was complete there. God had another assignment for me. When God releases us from something, it is a part of His divine purpose. This job was a part of my preparation for the next assignment. I took what I learned in that job and used it on the next one. If you are learning something new in a job, please be advised that God is going to use that new thing for His glory. I had to endure the preparation process. The new person (manager) was not there to stop my purpose but to prepare me for the many types of changes that I would face in life.

Change never comes easy, but it can be made easier if you accept the change for what it is and how it applies to your purpose. Reminder, God is the giver of purpose therefore workplace. We do not choose purpose. He places us in the workplace, and you (with free will) and He are the only two who can remove you; although some people really do believe they have that controlling power. God knows our thoughts. If a person has thoughts to fire you, God already knew about it. He can intervene at any given time. If God allows it to happen, then it was His will because He is never wrong concerning your life. Purpose is already attached to us. Everyone's footprint is different but testimonies help us to understand to see God's glory in our lives.

That workplace served two functions for that appointed time; preparation and push. Purpose existed long before the workplace was created, although man would really like to believe that they control that button! How wrong they are! God placed them there and those over them.

I found it interesting that one of the definitions of pain is described in Merriam-Webster [3] as, "Someone or something that causes trouble or makes you feel annoyed or angry." Whenever God wants to elevate you to your next level of purpose, most of the time He will use people and some pain. Elevation is testing ground. Your results to most of life's tests are directed by how you respond. This is why a lifestyle of prayer is so important. The more you talk to God, the more he will give you the answers to your test. Whatever workplace God has us in was designed by the Creator with a purpose in mind. When we truly understand who we work for, it will make our journey in life a lot easier. God gave each one of us life with a purpose and we are held accountable for that purpose, which means, everything we do in life, we have to give an account for. The workplace is no different than what we do in the home, church, school, community or anywhere we occupy.

To see your purpose, it takes vision. We have our physical eyes, but to see the purpose of your life requires spiritual insight. Prayer is the gateway to opening your spiritual understanding because it is the very thing that builds your relationship with God. Everything begins in the spirit before it is manifested in the natural. Thoughts, ideas, creations, discoveries, and inspirations all started in the spirit first. This is why there are new inventions and revelations manifesting daily. Technology is not new to God—we are just trying to catch up to get a glimpse of the extraordinary mind of God. We call technology "great," but God's thoughts have no boundaries, limitations, or failures.

Any company in operation originated from the spiritual thoughts of God, and every inch of it belongs to Him. I am so glad that His thoughts are not our thoughts (Isaiah 55:8). The Bible says that God knows the end before the beginning. This means everything that will be manifested on earth before the end of the earth as we know it has already happened in the spirit. What man could ever take credit for that? God already knows every company that ever existed or will exist in the future; He knows every business trade, and every exchange in the marketplace. God knows all of these things and more importantly He places us in a workplace to fulfill a purpose-driven assignment.

Just know that the counsel of God who knows everything is available and will stand forever. The way to receive His counsel is through prayer and having a relationship with Him is far better than any job or man could ever offer us.

> Remember the former things of old: for I am God, and there is none else; I am God, and there is none like me, Declaring the end from the beginning, and from ancient times the things that are not yet done, saying, My counsel shall stand, and I will do all my pleasure (Isaiah 46:9–10)

SEEING GOD'S VISION

You cannot see God's vision for your life without having a relationship with Him. In order to have a relationship with God, you have to talk to Him. Even Jesus prayed to God concerning his purpose while here on earth (Mathew 26:36, Luke 3:21; 11:1, etc.).

As I mentioned, we spend most of our waking hours in the workplace. Prayer is always needed where you dwell whether it is at home or at work. There are so many things that go on in the course of a work day. There are many things that are said in the course of a work day, and we must remember at all times that words have power. Have you ever thought about all the words that the atmosphere is being bombarded with? Can you imagine all that God hears?

Prayer works both ways. You can pray for yourself or others. We should be praying for both. The unique thing about the workplace is that the focus is not just on you. God's plan impacts all of us. So while you have a purpose and plan for your life, so does your coworker, family, and friends. What they do can impact you and vice versa. I found that some use the workplace as an exercise tool where they can flex their strength at work because they have little at home. Some use the workplace to hide who they really are, and then some use the workplace to help them get to the next level of their personal and spiritual goals.

Let's look at the life of Jacob when he worked for his uncle Laban. Jacob wrestled with purpose long before he wrestled with the angel of God. This setting is so common to working with family members in the workplace (spiritual and physical). Spiritual could be your church family and physical could represent working with your biological family. There are many Laban types in the world. They want to use your gifts and hold you hostage as long as they can to benefit themselves. Just a little background: Jacob flees his country after deceiving his brother for his birthright and his Father, Isaac's, blessing. He arrives at Haram and falls in love with Laban's daughter, Rachel, and offers to work for seven years to marry her.

After the seven years, Jacob's days are fulfilled, and he says to Laban, "Give me my wife."

Laban deceives Jacob by sending Leah (his older daughter) to him instead of Rachel, and he also gives Zilpah as the maid for Leah.

Jacob is upset as he is reaping deception and he ends up working another seven years to marry Rachel. Laban then gives Bilhah as the maid for Rachel. So Jacob ends up with four women and they all give birth to his children.

The Word of God tells us in Genesis 29:9 (NKJV) that Rachel was a shepherdess so she was known to work with the sheep but it does not state if that changed after she married. I can only imagine how the working environment could have been during those fourteen years. Jacob had a boss who deceived him but he still had to perform duties.

Whenever deception is the root, there will be chaos in the workplace. In Jacob's case he had his two legitimate wives, Leah and Rachel, plus two maids; however, his heart was with Rachel. The Word of God says in Genesis 29:31 that the Lord saw that Leah was unloved, so he opened her womb but made Rachel barren. Leah had four sons for Jacob and Rachel became envious. Envy is not one of the fruits of the spirit. Envy and strife belong to the enemy.

Acting under the influence of her emotions and being envious, Rachel said to Jacob, "Give me children, or else I die!"

This caused Jacob to get angry with Rachel. See the drama? These things had to impact on the workplace as well as their home.

Then to add more on top of that, Rachel sent her maid Bilhah to sleep with Jacob, and she had two sons. To add to that, Leah stopped bearing children, so she sent her maid Zilpah to Jacob, and she then bore two sons as well. After that, Leah had two more sons and a daughter by Jacob. Eventually, God remembered Rachel and opened her womb, and she finally bore a son, Joseph. Later, Rachel died giving birth to another son, named Benjamin. It's sad that she died during childbirth as that seemed to be her total focus and determination. In looking at this whole situation, one would think this is too much. Leah and Rachel were sisters, but it seems as though they acted like enemies. Layers of deceit were being applied, and Jacob was right in the middle of it. What started as deception with his very own brother followed him throughout his life while he worked for Laban, and it caused much pain.

Although Jacob was an excellent laborer and God blessed his hands indeed, there were some lessons to take away from this. Jacob thought he was working to get a wife, but the blessing was much bigger than that. When we are in a working environment, it can be so easy to lose focus on what the purpose of us being there is. It is always a greater purpose than what we see. Prayer changes the focus toward God, who has all the answers to everything we need.

Matthew 6:33 says, "But seek first the kingdom of God and His righteousness, and all these things shall be added to you." This is how God reveals things to us. If things are crazy on your job, what is the enemy trying to cover up? What is it that he does not want you to see or have? Chaos is merely a distraction to throw you off course. This is what was happening with Jacob. The emotional roller coaster with all the women was to distract him from the blessing. He asked for one woman, but he received four, and they each bore children. What he did not realize was all of this was a part of the blessing his father spoke unto him:

> May God Almighty bless you, and make you fruitful and multiply you, That you may be an assembly of peoples; And give you the blessing of Abraham, to you and your descendants with you, that you may inherit the land in which you are a stranger, Which God gave to Abraham. (Genesis 28:3–4)

Jacob received twelve sons and those children became the twelve tribes of Israel —this was part of his divine purpose.

More so, Jacob's encounter at Bethel (a place of God's presence) was also preparation for what was to come. He had a dream of the ladder that reached up into heaven and the Lord spoke to him with the declaration of the blessings for him and his descendants. Sometimes when we are in the mist of turmoil, we forget about the promises of God. When there is chaos all around us, we cannot think clearly and we tend to respond with emotions. However, God does not operate through our emotions. He is a spirit and I believe that's why He talks to us most of the time while we are asleep. When we are asleep, the things that hinder us when we are awake are removed, therefore God can talk to us by way of dream or audible conversation.

The workplace is a place of blessing and we need to see it from that perspective. The enemy knows that and he will do whatever he can to distract you for receiving your blessing. Sometimes others will be carrying your blessing, and you may meet them in the workplace. In the case of Jacob, each of those women carried his blessing. The boss was not a fair man, he had a spirit of greed and deception, but he had daughters and handmaidens to be used for the glory of God. Prayer does not always remove the plots and plans of the enemy but what it does is open your eyes to see the greater purpose. The more chaos on a job, the bigger the blessing, because the enemy is trying too hard to cover it up. He wants you to miss your blessing. I love how God uses even a job for His glory.

> But God hath chosen the foolish things of the world to confound the wise; and God hath chosen the weak things of the world to confound the things which are mighty (1 Corinthians 1:27)

Sometimes we wrestle with our purpose, meaning we may not want to accept the process that God takes us through. We sometimes want the short cut to get to the other side, but God is taking us through the process so we can learn how to keep the blessing when he gives it to us. Purpose is not always easy, but it is a perfect fit for our life. We were created with a purpose in mind, and God will use whosoever or whatsoever to complete His plan for our lives.

Kingdom prayers for the workplace and the laborers will keep the enemy on notice that no weapon formed against us will ever prosper. Prayer gives us a sound mind, and we need a sound mind while going through the process of life. When you pray, it is an elevated thought process; it moves you to an elevated level into the spirit. As long as the enemy can keep us focused on what we see in the natural (lower level), then we'll continue to dwell there in mind body and spirit. Prayer also brings peace in our spirit.

CHAPTER 4

SEASONS TELL TIME

CHAPTER 4

SEASONS TELL TIME

A season is referred to from a biblical fact as an appointed time in God.[4] We all have or will experience seasons in our lives. Those seasons are tied to our purpose and the plan God has established for us. All assignments have a beginning and end. God has designed our life assignments, which help shape our purpose here on earth. The beginning and end of those assignments has already been integrated into an appointed time or season. The Bible contains truth, and truth is what sets us free from the bondage of our own thinking. When we have been set free from captivity in our mind, we obtain rest in our spirit. I would rather have truth above anything else. Truth is a powerful pillar that stands when everything else falls.

Seasons are comparable because each season reveals the truth about a matter. A tree reveals the fruit in the appointed season, a flower reveals its bloom, and a babe reveals many seasons as he or she grows. Every event in your life happens within an appointed season. God created the seasons for us — they help us to identify the changes that become the milestones in our purpose-driven lives. Sometimes, a change in season can be more like a shift because it happens more suddenly than at other times. Every milestone is a mark in your life. Nothing in "this world" is perpetual or everlasting, and we will all have seasons with a beginning and ending.

Ecclesiastes summarize the different seasons. The scriptures outline the seasons by group, yet they are very different. Because there is no timeline for these seasons, you may find that as you experience one of them, you may experience the others as well.

> To everything there is a season, and a time to every purpose under the heaven:
> A time to be born, and a time to die; a time to plant, and a time to pluck up that which is planted;
> A time to kill, and a time to heal; a time to break down, and a time to build up;
> A time to weep, and a time to laugh; a time to mourn, and a time to dance;
> A time to cast away stones, and a time to gather stones together; a time to embrace, and a time to refrain from embracing;
> A time to get, and a time to lose; a time to keep, and a time to cast away;
> A time to rend, and a time to sew; a time to keep silence, and a time to speak;
> A time to love, and a time to hate; a time of war, and a time of peace.
> (Ecclesiastes 3:1–8)

Because the Bible is specific in calling out the seasons respectively, I wanted to focus on each one of the seasons in verses 1-8. Some of the illustrations shared in this chapter are from revealed experiences, but as you read through each one, you may find how your own experiences map back to certain seasons in the workplace.

1: To everything there is a season, and a time to every purpose under the heaven:

A Time to Every Purpose

The scripture above tells us that there is a time for everything and a season for every activity under the heavens. In every job we have ever held, in every workplace, everything includes seasons, and those seasons are tied to your life's timeline. Every phase that a person can experience during their season in the workplace can be found in the scriptures. Psalms 119:105 says, "Thy word is a lamp unto my feet, and a light unto my path," meaning the Bible sheds light or revelation on every area and every experience in life. I have personally found this to be true. Ecclesiastes 1:9 says it better:

> The thing that hath been, it is that which shall be; and that which is done is that which shall be done: and there is no new thing under the sun. (Ecclesiastes 1:9)

The Bible is full of words of wisdom that we can all mediate on. If we allow the Word of God to be the light in our lives, then our understanding of our purpose will have more clarity than ever imagined. Just as the Bible contains this information about the seasons, there is another scripture that says it is not for us to know the seasons or times.

> And he said unto them, It is not for you to know the times or the seasons, which the Father hath put in his own power. (Acts 1:7)

Just like the disciples, we want to know the times or dates of events, but God, the Creator, is the master timekeeper for all events, situations, and circumstances. He wants us to have knowledge of what the seasons are, as pointed out in Ecclesiastes 3, but not to know the actual start and finish date or time within each season. God is eternal meaning everlasting without any constraints of timelines. We cannot box God into man's timings; he determines our timing within our seasons. We have to simply trust God and His infinite wisdom that He makes everything beautiful in His own time.

> He hath made everything beautiful in his time: also he hath set the world in their heart, so that no man can find out the work that God maketh from the beginning to the end. (Ecclesiastes 3:11)

The next portion of this chapter will walk through each of the seasons outlined in the scriptures above. As I began to write about each one, the Holy Spirit shone a light on each one for the purpose of this book; however, there are even more revelations to discover as you read through each one because they pertain to your walk through life. I am sure many of you have gone through different seasons in your lifespan—therefore, you should be able to relate to them as being an appointed time not chosen by ourselves. As we expound on these outlined seasons, you will find biblical and personal experiences to better connect the life application of seasons.

2: A time to be born, and a time to die; a time to plant, and a time to pluck up that which is planted;

A Time to Be Born

To be born is the most amazing, phenomenal and extraordinary process ever created. It is truly fascinating when you think of every unique timing of a birth that only God could have created. The exclusive design of the overarching process before the actual birthing happens is beyond man's unfolding wisdom. Man can take no credit for any portion of God's recipe for life. Each footprint in life is different, and all have seasons that are tied to a purpose. We have no need to ever worry about when someone is to be born because the timeline has already been established long before the season occurs. The seasons we go through are built within the timeline of life.

The word born is defined as "brought into life by the process of birth" as well as, according to Merriam-Webster, "destined from." [5]To be "destined from" means "meant to be, fate, or predestined." We have all been destined to be born according to the Creator's plan.[6] The Hebrew word for born is yalad (yaw-lad), and it means "to bear, bring forth, to beget"[7]—basically the word denotes the action of giving birth: bearing children. Naturally, if you are reading this, you have already gone through the literal process of being physically born, so let's talk about the season.

As mentioned earlier, God has created all of us for a divine purpose. God knew us before we were born; therefore, we all have a purpose for being born. There is a great example in the Book of Jeremiah that tells us that God had a plan for us before we are even born. All of us may not be prophets, but we all have a divine purpose.

> Then the word of the Lord came unto me, saying, Before I formed thee in the belly I knew thee; and before thou camest forth out of the womb I sanctified thee, and I ordained thee a prophet unto the nations. (Jeremiah 1:4–5)

Here are a few more scriptures we can reference:

> According as he hath chosen us in him before the foundation of the world, that we should be holy and without blame before him in love. (Ephesians 1:4)

> Listen, O isles, unto me; and hearken, ye people, from far; The Lord hath called me from the womb; from the

bowels of my mother hath he made mention of my name. (Isaiah 49:1)

But when it pleased God, who separated me from my mother's womb, and called me by his grace, to reveal his Son in me, that I might preach him among the heathen; immediately I conferred not with flesh and blood. (Galatians 1:15–16)

Between the times we are born, and when we die, there is a tremendous process that takes place. Some were born for specific assignments that impact the human race in diverse ways. Certainly, Adam had a direct foundational impact on all of us. He was "the first born," and he can be considered as the first laborer. One of his duties was to name every living creature, and he worked in the garden of Eden (Genesis 2). Adam's life process set the standard for our role of workmanship. He lived for 930 years, and we can only imagine how many seasons of diversity he endured throughout his lifetime. Adam's purpose was great, and there was only one that had an even greater impact on the human race: Jesus.

In an appointed season in Adam's life, he received a son and named him Cain. Then in another season, Abel was born. Cain and Abel both had job assignments. Cain was a tiller of the ground. Abel was the keeper of sheep—two separate laborers working in different capacities, but driven by the same purpose. We can have different workplaces, but they can still be tied to the same purpose. We were all born with different gifts. Therefore we have different assignments. Cain's assignment had a different process to Abel's, but ultimately, they were both required to produce fruit.

No matter what our work assignments are, we are all required to produce fruit. Another important key we don't want to miss in viewing this biblical principle is that all work should be done unto the Lord. The earth is His and the fullness thereof. Everything belongs to God, and every job is formed from God's creation. This alone should set some people's minds free when struggling with money. If Cain and Abel understood the principle of giving God an offering, we should have the same understanding without rebuttal.

Timing is everything. From the time we are born, we are being trained to produce fruit. This is why it is so important that we train a child to follow the correct path, as mentioned in Proverbs 22:6. However, I like Ephesians 6:4 more: "Bring them up in the training and instruction of the Lord." Cain and Abel were both trained in the instruction of the Lord to work and produce fruit unto God.

Genesis 4:3 tells us that in the process of time Cain brought an offering of the fruit of the ground to the Lord. His brother Abel also brought the Lord fat from the firstborn of his flock. The fat was considered the best part of the animal and the firstborn's fat was even better. It is all about the delivery of what we are presenting to God. Not only did they Cain and Abel understand the principle of giving back to God, but more so the timing of offering up their fruit. They were not late in their delivery. Are we presenting our best from the fruit of our labor and at the time we should? God accepted Abel's offering but rejected Cain's. This caused Cain to become angry. How many times have we become angry because someone else in the workplace received recognition, promotion or more fruit (pay)?

I had to learn that promotion comes from God. Most of the time it comes when we are not looking for it.

Now that the physical part of being born has been talked about; there is a spiritual perspective as well. Although the Old Testament reasoning is directed toward the physical, I believe that the spiritual perspective is just as significant as we are made of both flesh and spirit as indicated in the scripture below:

> That which is born of the flesh is flesh; and that which is born of the Spirit is spirit. (John 3:6)

One may ask how these things tie into your seasons in the workplace. Once we understand spiritual things and the mysteries of God, we can map them to every area of our lives. As we understand the methodology of seasons, it causes us to grow beyond earthly things to receive the wisdom of heavenly things. The Bible is full of wisdom, and this knowledge is free and available to all that receive it.

The workplace is only part of our purpose, but a very important part; it plays out the script in our lives. I share Bible evidence and demonstration as well as my experiences to help bring understanding of what God has revealed. The Bible is a book of testimonies with the great wisdom to aid with understanding of spiritual things. Our faith, hope, and belief gives us access to greater things. What could be greater than everlasting life? If we believe in the word of testimonies in the Bible, we obtain life forever. Worldly knowledge is limited because it only exists in the world, but what happens when we leave this world? This is where true wisdom comes in. For if we know this physical life will end, then hope do we have? Jesus offers us hope through believing that he was sent from our Father in heaven to save us, and through his life, we can have everlasting life, which builds our faith in our daily walk. More so, God did not leave us helpless after Jesus left his physical life —he left us with the Holy Spirit, which uses whosoever with revealed knowledge to continue to help others. My writing goes beyond just being an author: part of my purpose is to allow the Holy Spirit to use me to help others.

Being born again is a revealed knowledge. Jesus shared this knowledge with a man named Nicodemus who was a part of the Pharisees ruling council. Nicodemus's position could be compared with our US Supreme Court. The ruling council in those days would handle civil and theological concerns. They followed the Old Testament laws and religious traditions. Jesus often challenged their views, therefore posing a threat to their council-ship and the way they ruled from a governmental perspective. Jesus's teachings began to open the minds of the people. When our minds are renewed to a different way of thinking, it poses a threat to the enemy and old ways of thinking. Negativity is the first objective of the enemy. The Pharisees, as we know, was not fond of Jesus, nor his teaching. When the truth of God is revealed it will bear witness to your spirit.

Typically, we know the truth when we hear it, but when our heart is hardened and not open, we won't receive it, and will reject it instead. Nicodemus had an open heart to explore more of the truth. He visited Jesus after hours so that the other Pharisees would not see him. I would say he was a man seeking greater wisdom. He addressed Jesus as rabbi, which means "teacher" (one respected) and also acknowledged how no man could perform the miracles Jesus could unless God was with him. Jesus answered Nicodemus with one of his most perplexing statements:

> Jesus answered and said unto him, Verily, verily, I say unto thee, Except a man be born again, he cannot see the kingdom of God. (John 3:3)

This was a deep speech then and still is today. When Jesus said, "Except a man," he referred to all people being able to enter into God's Kingdom, not just the Jews. Remember: John 3:16 says that God so loved the world (all of us) He gave His only Son for whosoever could have everlasting life. This includes all mankind. All of us must be born again to live forever in God's Kingdom. Nicodemus response was:

> How can a man be born when he is old? Can he enter the second time into his mother's womb, and be born? (John 3:4)

Like Nicodemus, our initial thought is that born refers to a physical activity. We are not wrong, but carnal thinking in a spiritual conversation will lead us immediately to the flesh versus the spiritual. Like many of us, we forget quickly when we are talking to or hearing from someone who is sent by God.

> Jesus answered, Verily, verily, I say unto thee, Except a man be born of water and of the Spirit, he cannot enter into the kingdom of God. That which is born of the flesh is flesh; and that which is born of the Spirit is spirit. (John 3:5–6)

Jesus knew his words troubled Nicodemus, so right away he addressed it and gave the parable about the wind blowing. For we know that the wind blows, but we cannot explain how and where it blows. We can hear it at times and feel it but cannot determine its origin or destiny. This is how being born of the spirit is. We cannot explain every detail about it, but it exists. When we begin to receive more of the things of God, it is like the wind blowing in our lives—a regeneration or rebirthing happens in the spirit. It gives us spiritual insight as refreshing as water that fulfills a thirst deep within. As we learn more of the mysteries of God, we can walk in a new light of revelation. Being born again spiritually is that new life and a closer walk with God.

> Marvel not that I said unto thee, Ye must be born again. The wind bloweth where it listeth, and thou hearest the sound thereof, but canst not tell whence it cometh, and whither it goeth: so is every one that is born of the Spirit. (John 3:7–8)

We should all desire to be born again of the spirit. As we live out this life in the workplace, or any place, a renewed mind and view of spiritual things help us in our understanding of our purpose. The truth not only helps us to be born again, but to set us free to believe in life everlasting. In every season and every opportunity, believe in this truth, the only begotten Son:

> For God so loved the world, that he gave his only begotten Son, that whosoever believeth in him should not perish, but have everlasting life. For God sent not his Son into the world to condemn the world; but that the world through him might be saved. (John 3:16)

A Time to Die

We all have this appointed time. Whether we want to believe it or not, this time will greet us all, and our work on this earth will be finished. As a result, Cain killed his brother, and this was the first mention of murder in the Bible. Abel's life was short lived, but nevertheless, God allowed it to happen—because it was tied to his purpose. God is the master timekeeper of our lives. Birth and death are appointed times. What we learn from the process is that God allows us to go through certain things because it is entwined with our destiny. Things are not always pretty or completely understood when they happen, but God is fully aware, and these things are already on His timeline. A time to live and a time to die are both appointed times. Isaiah says that God is the stability of our times.

> And He will be the security and stability of your times, a treasure of salvation, wisdom and knowledge. (Isaiah 33:6 AMP)

As much as we want to control our time, we cannot. All we can do is make the best out of the time God gives us, above all being a laborer unto the Lord. Our work time is precious because it is the part of the process of the production of our fruit. We want God to accept our fruit that comes from our time here on the earth before we die.

Whatever fruit we produce in the process of our life is an offering unto the Lord, from the time we are born to the time we die. In the workplace, we must remember who our real employer is; this helps free me in my thinking and reminds me of my everyday purpose for being in my job. Everything we do at work is being captured by God because it is a product of our fruit. God revealed to me that whatever fruit I was producing was being offered to Him: my attendance, attitude, how I treated coworkers, my efforts and work ethics—but most of all my conversation. All these things produce fruit.

Our conversation is a very strong fruit. Our words have the power to speak into the atmosphere —like the one who we are made in the image of. We do not have the same power as God; however, our words do have the power to change things. For this reason, Satan continues to entice us to say things that will promote negativity in the atmosphere. Our conversation plays a major role in our lives—another reason why prayer is so important. Producing fruit applies to every type of workplace. As a check point throughout our life, we should continually ask ourselves, "What fruit am I offering up to God?"

It is interesting that before Abel murdered Cain, the Lord talked to him, asking him why he was angry. Although God knew the answer, He still asked. When God asks you questions, it is not for God; it is for you. If you can answer the question, you will give thought to your answer. Whatever Cain's response was, God wanted him to know that if he did well (with a true heart), then he would accept what was offered to him. However, if you do not do this, then sin will be waiting at the door. This was a warning. I believe that God always presents warnings to us. Evil exists long before it happens; our thoughts form things in our hearts first. Satan's desire is for you to sin, especially against God so he can sift you as wheat.

> And the Lord said, Simon, Simon, behold, Satan hath desired to have you, that he may sift you as wheat. (Luke 22:31)

One of our most important goals in life is never to allow Satan to rule over us. Abel was murdered by his brother. This type of sin is severe. There are many types of sin, but murder is a sin that can never be reversed. Bloodshed is viewed as horrific and very painful to whoever is impacted by it. I have to wonder why Cain would choose such to kill his brother when it is such a permanent act. When the influence of sin rests in our hearts, it can cause us to make choices and perform acts under that evil spirit. Most murders are formed in the mind and played out there before they are even executed. If Satan can influence your mind, the sifting process can take place, and your thoughts of good, righteousness, joy, forgiveness, and most of all, love can be separated from you like the wheat from the chaff.

There have been many cases of murder in the workplace. My heart goes out to those impacted by those horrendous acts led by Satan. Some people do not have a relationship with God and have not experienced the true gift of love that bears all things. I'd like to draw attention to one emotion in particular, called "anger," which is a kindled fire. This is a strong spirit, but love is by far stronger than all. If we sought more love in the world, there would be fewer murders. We have to be ever so careful of our thoughts, especially when people mistreat us, knock us down or shoot fiery darts at our back. When these spirits rise up (and they will) in the workplace, it is imperative that we pray on-demand and seek to love rather than hate, no matter of the circumstance or how hard it is. It takes some practice, but it can be done.

Thoughts are the spearheads of good and evil. They are directional, meaning each spear leads you in a certain direction. Thoughts can create good acts, but they can also craft very dangerous acts. Continuously entertained evil thoughts can create a spark—one that can start a fire. If Satan can spark a fire, he will; but his ultimate goal is to generate a wildfire that is out of control. His fuel is hot and full of destruction. Do not play with it or underestimate its heat. Prayer is the fire prevention in the workplace. Praying without ceasing is forever needed in any workplace to help prevent satanic attacks that lead to physically hurting others and murders in the workplace.

The workplace is always a target for our enemy. Again, this is where you spend most of your time; therefore, where you produce most of your fruit and what is being offered up to God. For a long time, I thought the only thing I was offering God was money. I was so wrong in my thinking.

We are fighting kingdom wars especially in the workplace. Kingdom wars are battles against the kingdom of God. Here is a wake-up call—Satan does not want you to be added to the kingdom God, but rather he wants you to spend eternity with Him. So everything he is pitching at you is against the kingdom of God. Some workplace wars have been going on for years. It is time for those wars to die! Jesus has already won every battle for us. Satan's job is to keep you from believing that truth by ensuring you do not understand this fact. When this happens, we continue to war against one another time after time. The enemy knows as long as there are fires in our thoughts, we cannot produce good fruit.

Prayer is a kingdom practice. This is one of the most important tools you have to fight against the wiles of the devil. Prayer changes things, especially our thoughts. This is a proven method! Think about it: when you talk to God, do you tell Him how bad you want to thrash someone, tear them apart, knock them down or keep them from getting ahead? No, you do not. You try to hide that from God—as if you really can. Those inward thoughts are manufactured from the enemy. God wants you to talk to Him so he can change your thoughts—so the battle can die. If you can kick-start your day with a little prayer, it can move mountains that have hindered your production of fruit for years.

In this murder case of Cain and Abel, anger may have been the root, but I believe that other spirits fueled that situation, like jealously, hatred, animosity, resentment and, most of all, covetousness. We see a lot of evil in the workplace, just as Cain and Abel did. The murder happened in the field, which can be considered Cain's workplace since his job was a tiller of the ground. Nevertheless, God allowed the carnage to happen between them. This was Abel's appointed time to die. As a keepsake, we all have that divine appointment with God.

> Thus speaketh the Lord of hosts, saying, Execute true judgment, and shew mercy and compassions every man to his brother: And oppress not the widow, nor the fatherless, the stranger, nor the poor; and let none of you imagine evil against his brother in your heart. (Zechariah 7:9–10)

There are other things in our lives that have a time die. Bad thoughts should die daily. We can pull down those evil imaginations that promote fires and let them die. Some of us have trespasses against one another and have been at war for too long—let it die today. This message is a reminder of how important the workplace is because it is the place where we produce the fruit of our labor. Sin will always be lying at the door, especially in the workplace. It takes on many forms within the people we work with. We are all there to produce fruit, but more importantly, we must understand who the fruit belongs to. From the time we are born to the time we die, we all have a workplace, and it is driven by our purpose to multiply and bear fruit.

A Time to Plant

This season is very similar to the previous seasons: a time to be born and a time to die. Before something can be born, a seed is planted, and when someone dies, it is like something being uprooted. This season can be also related to good and evil. In the workplace, you can experience good, and on the other hand, you can experience evil. All depends on what is being planted and what is sprouts.

In this context, the Hebrew word for plant is nata, which means "to strike in; fastened." [8]The first mention of the word planted is in Genesis 2:8, as it references God planting a garden. The word is also used symbolically for planting people. Merriam-Webster refers to plant as most of us do: "to put a seed in the ground to grow." When you plant something, you are placing it into something. God planted a garden in Eden and He put man in the garden to work and take care of it. Labor and the workplace was introduced at the beginning and it was referred to as "a garden." God created the garden and made every tree grow to produce food for man before He placed man in it. This tells us that the garden was created for man, rather than man being created for the garden (job). When God places us in a job, it already exists before we start laboring there. Everything God does, He does in order. We are in our jobs because God placed us there. For this reason, our jobs are a blessing and we should thank God daily for our workplace. Think about it: God planted a business idea in someone to develop a company just so you could be blessed. Every workplace started with a purpose and a plan. The idea was planted within a human being, then it was nurtured and matured to become a workplace for others to be sown into. God is so awesome and he is still planting business ideas today.

The planting season is a critical time. There are so many factors to consider when planting. First, you must recognize that God has given you a favorable place to plant your time, gifts, good deeds, and seeds. These are all foundational ingredients for planting. The planting ingredients exist within us and are also tied to our purpose to be used for God's glory.

I like the planting season because it is the beginning of something new. God has planted me in several different workplaces in my lifetime. Each place had a season that was applied to my life. I have to admit that I did not always appreciate the purpose of me being there. The starting point at the planting was always good, but as the process continued, my view changed about being planted there. Sometimes we forget about how the growing process works. We get comfortable and lose the excitement of when we were first planted. After planting there comes the nurturing and watering. As we grow, we start looking at other plants around us, and depending on who we are having conversations with, it can cause us to not want to endure the growth process. Our patience can wear thin, and we can go into a place of complacency where self-satisfaction enters in. God is the overseer, and He is watching our fruits manifest.

I recall having a part-time job as a waitress to earn extra money to help with my daughter's college tuition. It was a fast-paced restaurant, and I thought it would be a piece of cake.

I remember saying, "This will be easy; I will run circles around these other servers." I had already sized them up before I started working.

The planting season began, and after being in training for a week or so, I kept telling them I was ready to take large parties by myself. I saw how others were making good tips and I wanted them too.

I kept asking, and eventually, the manager said. "Okay, Rhonda, go for it."

It was a Friday night, and the restaurant was jammed with people inside and out. My section was overflowing with people, and I did not have any help. It was a mess! It turned out to be the worst night of my waitressing career. I had large table parties of people, and they placed very complex orders and continued to request drink refills like there was a drought. It became overwhelming, and I forgot some of the orders and food got cold, which upset my customers; not to mention, the cook was mad at me for having to remake orders. I felt so bad and did not make many tips after all. My eyes were on the wrong prize. Please hear me—money cannot be the reason for the season. I had the will power to be a larger plant, but I was missing some main ingredients needed to help me grow to produce good fruit. When God plants us, He will give us the technique or skill needed for the work.

Basic nurturing ingredients are key in the planting season for the workplace: listening, observing, studying your skill and being focused on the real reason for being there. Many times, we do not wait through the nurturing process to strengthen our roots. This process is to prepare us for each phase of His planting season. My manager knew that I was not ready, but gave me room to learn this valuable lesson for myself.

The end result was that over time, I ended up being one of the top servers, making very good tips. I also learned to respect the work that servers do. They interact with many types of people, and there is always something God is trying to show you about people when you are working in this type of environment. We can miss it if we are not careful. We cannot be focused on the monetary perspective. Even with tipping, because God is watching to see how you handle the money He has given you. Today I still use some of the principles learned from that job. God multiplied my fruit, and after my season was up at that workplace, He planted me somewhere else.

There are seasons (appointed times) for us to be in a particular workplace (garden) to plant or to sow. When we are laboring in the workplace, we are sowing seeds to produce a harvest. We are using our God-given talents and gifts when we put our hands to labor. Granted, there are many different types of jobs that utilize all types of skillsets but the end result is to multiply fruit that will continue the production cycle. We all have a purpose for being on a job no matter where God plants the garden.

A Time to Pluck

There are seasons to plant and there are seasons to pluck up. Everything we plant should represent our Father in heaven. Jesus spoke about the results of plants not planted for God in the parable about defilement. In our workplace, we want to plant good seeds so that what is produced is good.

> He replied, "Every plant that my heavenly Father has not planted will be pulled up by the roots."
> (Matthew 5:13)

The Hebrew word for pluck is aqar (aw-kar), which means "root; to tear away; root-out"; other references figuratively used "to move, remove, and separate forcibly or abruptly."[9] The uniqueness of plucking is that God will use us to continue planting good so it can be multiplied throughout the season.[10] However, if bad or evil exist, he is the one that plucks it up. Anything that contaminates the roots cannot grow into anything good. If there is evil being sown in the workplace, do not be dismayed. That season is short lived and God will surely pluck it up in the appointed time. God is not mocked. Whatsoever a man sow, that shall he reap.

> Thus saith the Lord, the God of Israel; Like these good figs, so will I acknowledge them...for their good. For I will set mine eyes upon them for good...and I will build them, and not pull them down; and I will plant them, and not pluck them up. (Jeremiah 24:5–6)

In the Old Testament scripture above, God uses the parable of the figs to the prophet Jeremiah to reference the message about planting and plucking up. At the beginning of chapter 24, God showed Jeremiah a vision of two baskets of figs that were set before the temple. Being set before the temple symbolizes acceptance to God. One basket had good figs, and the other had bad figs that could not be eaten. In the natural fruit is only good if it can be eaten. Bad fruit is waste and cannot be used.

The season referenced in this chapter was after Nebuchadnezzar, the King of Babylon, had carried the son of the

King of Judah, the princes, and the craftsmen and smiths from Jerusalem into captivity. These are laborers (good fruit) being uprooted from one workplace to another. Others were not taken from Jerusalem but remained in the land in their sin. The metaphor was showing the separation of good and evil. God accepts what is good. Even though some were placed in captivity (another workplace), it was for their good.

Do not be upset when God separates you from a workplace. He knows the end from the beginning. We cannot see that far down the road, but God always has a plan. Sometimes God will change your work location but is not for you to panic about. If you did not do anything within your power to change your work location, then rest assured that it was a God move.

In this case, the others (represented as bad figs that could not be eaten) who remained in Jerusalem and in the land of Egypt would endure trouble, and God would send the sword, the famine and the pestilence among them until they were consumed by the land that God blessed them with.

> And as the evil figs, which cannot be eaten, they are so evil; surely thus saith the Lord, So will I give Zedekiah the king of Judah, and his princes, and the residue of Jerusalem, that remain in this land, and them that dwell in the land of Egypt: And I will deliver them to be removed into all the kingdoms of the earth for their hurt, to be a reproach and a proverb, a taunt and a curse, in all places whither I shall drive them. And I will send the sword, the famine, and the pestilence, among

them, till they be consumed from off the land that I gave unto them and to their fathers. (Jeremiah 24:8–10)

As we see, work and fruit are very important to God, which is why there are appointed times for both. For this reason, it is very important that we plant good seeds to produce good fruit in our jobs. The planting and plucking season will always remain as long as the earth exists.

While the earth remaineth, seedtime and harvest, and cold and heat, and summer and winter, and day and night shall not cease. (Genesis 8:22)

No matter how we are treated in the workplace, it is still important to produce good. We all belong to God's garden, and everything we say and do is accounted for.

We have to give an account not only for our actions but for our words as well. Words are seeds, and those seeds can germinate; meaning take root, live, and grow. The outcome of that root is determined by the seed that is planted. Our conversation in the workplace is key to the outcome of our actions. I realize it is hard to be responsible for every word we say, but they are seeds, and when seeds are watered in the due season, it can bring forth fruit. The goal is to make sure our fruit arrives in the good basket to be acceptable to God.

> But I say unto you, That every idle word that men shall speak, they shall give account thereof in the day of judgment. For by thy words thou shalt be justified, and by thy words thou shalt be condemned. (Matthew 12:36–37)

3: A time to kill, and a time to heal; a time to break down, and a time to build up;

A Time to Kill

This season is unparalleled in the sense of its effects being completely opposite to one another. Something that dies is rarely healed in the natural. To kill something stops the life of a thing, but to heal continues the life of a thing. More so, both seasons are somewhat sensitive to survey as it pertains to the workplace.

We know that the sixth commandment says thou shall not kill, which refers to murder. To be clear, in this text Ecclesiastes 3:3, referencing a time to kill is not referring to a time to murder or slaughter a person. The scripture refers to a time or season to kill something: that something is likely a sin. Merriam-Webster has many definitions of the word kill, one being, "to put an end to [something]." To kill sin means "to put to an end or deprive it of life within you."[11]

As it pertains to our subject of the workplace, in meditating on this one more, it was revealed that this season has a more of a prophetic (divinatory) meaning than some of the other seasons. The prophetic draws us to an extensive view of a message and is usually pointing to Christ. The Bible illustrates how Jesus encountered both appointed times. The sins of mankind were killed when Jesus died on the cross; he bore our sins in his body on that cross. This was done so that we would not have to endure the chastisement deserving of our sins: Christ took the death sentence for us. This death sentence refers to eternal punishment (in hell), which is the wages of sin.

> For the wages of sin is death; but the gift of God is eternal life through Jesus Christ our Lord. (Romans 6:23)

> And these shall go away into everlasting punishment: but the righteous into life eternal. (Matthew 25:46)

For this reason, we should make every effort to kill sin in our lives. As hard as this may seem to accomplish, being dead to sin in every part of our body (including our mouth) gives access to being alive in Christ. Sin cannot dwell in eternal life with God—it separates us from Him.

> Likewise reckon ye also yourselves to be dead indeed unto sin, but alive unto God through Jesus Christ our Lord. Let not sin therefore reign in your mortal body, that ye should obey it in the lusts thereof. Neither yield ye your members as instruments of unrighteousness unto sin: but yield yourselves unto God, as those that are alive from the dead, and your members as instruments of righteousness unto God. (Romans 6:11–13)

Jesus dying on a cross represents the killing of sin from a much bigger perspective.

> Who his own self bare our sins in his own body on the tree, that we, being dead to sins, should live unto righteousness: by whose stripes ye were healed. (1 Peter 2:24)

God could have used whatever He wanted, but his body was used. Major revelation here: our bodies have a significant purpose. Jesus's body was used not only to save us, but also to heal us! When we are dead unto sin we can live righteously. If we live righteously, we can have everlasting life with God.

Sin can attach itself to flesh through our desires, thoughts, and actions to name a few. Jesus was nailed to the cross by the flesh. He was the only one worthy to take on that great task for mankind because he was sinless. He was dead to sin in his body and he bore all the intense torture to his flesh. As a result, all of our sins were supernaturally nailed to that cross by way of Jesus's flesh, therefore killing sin. He was not murdered, but he laid down his life for us. Jesus spoke this prophetically before he was taken to the cross.

> The reason my Father loves me is that I lay down my life—only to take it up again. No one takes it from me, but I lay it down of my own accord. I have authority to lay it down and authority to take it up again. This command I received from my Father. (John 10:17 NIV)

His death was for a divine purpose. Even being raised from the dead (healing) was for an even greater purpose.

> We are witnesses of everything he did in the country of the Jews and in Jerusalem. They killed him by hanging him on a cross, but God raised him from the dead on the third day and caused him to be seen. (Acts 10:39–40 NIV)

Before Jesus was taken to the cross, he was found in the Garden of Gethsemane. I found this to be a metaphor for the workplace—the garden could be considered a place where work was being performed. In this garden, he was praying so hard that his soul was exceeding sorrowful. Luke 22:44 describes Jesus's sweat while praying as great drops of blood falling down to the ground. Depending on the nature of the work, it can cause a person to sweat. Remember also how God does extraordinary things in a garden. Most movies I have seen do not make this particular garden (Gethsemane) very attractive as I imagine the garden of Eden was, nevertheless the work being done in Gethsemane was just as relevant and important as the work in Eden; just as some workplaces have beautiful surroundings and some are not a delightful place to work in. Nevertheless, that garden was chosen as a designated place to be used by Jesus to demonstrate his posture in prayer before the most significant event that ever happened to mankind. We all have our garden (workplace) where God wants to use us.

The sins of the whole world were put on Jesus. Only Christ could bear our sins. This may be hard for some to comprehend because God's thoughts and ways are far deeper than we can ever imagine. I am so thankful that God loves all of us so much that He sent His Son to do this for us. Because of Christ, our sins are forgiven, and we have regained our rights back with God that were lost during the fall of Adam. These rights are the opportunity to have everlasting life with God. Therefore, the results of this great accomplishment mean we can have a choice to choose everlasting life versus eternal judgment. This was a time to kill so that mankind could have the opportunity to be healed. Jesus predicted this would happen.

> And they shall kill him, and the third day he shall be raised again. (Matthew 17:23)

Even though we can be forgiven of our sins, sin still exists in the world. Because sin exists, there are still appointed times when we can kill the sin in our lives. Peter teaches about abstaining from sinful desires. We abstain by killing sin at the very root. Sinful desires begin with a thought, then they take root so they can wage war against our soul through our heart. Once our heart is out of tune with Christ, we indulge in earthly desires that can lead to sin. The real question for me is, do I allow sin to kill me, or do I kill the sin in my life?

Peter also refers to believers as strangers and pilgrims, which means aliens or visitors of this world. We believers are passing through this earth to get to our real home with our heavenly Father. Everything on this earth is temporary and will soon pass away. It is vitally important to remove any residue of sin from our lives because it cannot be attached to us in eternity; it cannot exist there. But the spirit lives forever. In the book of 2 Corinthians 5:1–3, it talks about how when our earthly body is dissolved we have another building in eternity. This is our heavenly body that will last forever.

A time to kill is like a checkpoint season for deleting things in your life that can kill your purpose in the workplace or the destiny God has for you. A lot of things can happen in the workplace throughout seasons. Evil exists whether we want it to or not. Sometimes we can see evil manifesting to take you out, and other times it can be a silent killer. The silent killers are the sins working behind the scenes, forming weapons to attack you when you least expect.

You can tell when your season is about to change—the enemy turns up the volume. The Word of God says our enemy walks the earth seeking whom he can devour, meaning he is seeking who he can use to destroy what God has for you. Whenever God is getting ready to promote you, the enemy will send something or someone with a plan of derailment to obstruct the progress. The devil cannot take your promises that God has for you, but what he does is get you to forfeit them. When you forfeit something, you lose the right to it by some form of error or offense (in this case sin).

When people come up against you in the workplace, you must remember they are being used. And believe me, the devil is aiming for a two-for-one deal: destroy you and the one he is using. However, if you focus on God and resist the devil, he will flee.

> Be sober, be vigilant; because your adversary the devil, as a roaring lion, walketh about, seeking whom he may devour. (1 Peter 5:8)

> Submit yourselves therefore to God. Resist the devil, and he will flee from you. (James 4:7)

When the volume turns up in the workplace, take inventory of everything around you that could be attached to sin. God is good and merciful and He gives us room to get it right. Conviction starts in our heart, and that opens the door to forgiveness, repentance, and the outpouring of more love. Everything that is good is wrapped in love, including your workplace. That's how God delivers it to us. We cannot do anything good without love being involved. Selah. It is the love of God that is in us that allows us the ability to love. God is love and He shares that love with each one of us. We have a place on earth because He loves us. Everything we have, originated because of love.

Before you can kill the sin, you have to first discern that sin exists. It will be exposed because sin cannot remain hidden, and this is why it is necessary to pray for your workplace. There are no formula words for talking to God about what He is revealing to you. Praying to God is heart-to-heart. Remember He holds the keys to your heart and understands every area of your life. He is waiting to hear your voice. Here are a few helpful steps to killing sin in the workplace:

> **K**eep your eyes on the things of God, therefore life
> **I**gnore words that do not bear fruit
> **L**ove no matter what the enemy throws at you
> **L**ift up your voice to praise God no matter what season you are in
>
> **S**peak words of life and not death

Invoke daily prayer for strength against the enemy's attack in the workplace
Never give up on God because he won't give up on you

A Time to Heal

There is a season to heal according to Ecclesiastes 3:4. The Hebrew word for heal is raphah (raw-faw), which means "to mend, to heal, to restore to normal." [12]God performs the act of healing based on our belief, and according to Strong's Concordance. Healing is needed not only where sickness exists but in other areas as well. Those parts that need healing could be from past hurts, from words that have scared us, a loss of a loved one, or from physical recovery; nevertheless, God has appointed a season to heal. In our workplaces we can endure trauma in many forms. In some cases, it can be more severe than others. Distress, anguish, torture can all wound us to the point where healing need be applied. All the things I mention can be characterized as evil fruit—they are not the fruit of the spirit, and therefore the author of those things is Satan. Have you noticed that whenever Satan tries to plot against you, God has a solution to overturn him?

Healing is designed for us. Jesus demonstrated healing by being raised from the dead, and there were many other acts of healing throughout the Bible. To have a season set aside to heal is a great asset to life. I can understand why it is a season, because healing can be a process. Some processes take longer than others. This is covered in more detail later.

This season is important because sometimes we do not realize how much we need to heal from the impacts of life. The workplace is only one complex place; at times, there can be so much chaos going on in our workplace with persecution and suffering, that it gives us a newfound respect for what Jesus really did for us. I know that sounds extreme but—indicating contrast—it becomes an opportunity to be raised up and healed by the hand of God. Healing can be manifested in different ways, and God's timing for healing is perfect. Personally, I think

God places us in certain seasons at times so we can see some of what He sees. Can you imagine all the things that God sees every day? We would not be able to function or digest some of the things that go on behind the scenes that God hides from us.

When your workplace is in a chaotic state, God has a way of shifting your season so that you can heal. This is why it is important to recognize your seasons. When you recognize your season and understand that it is a part of a purpose, you won't rebel against it.

The hardest part about being in a certain season is the waiting. We are such a microwave generation: we want it now! But we have to wait because the process is not finished. I know God raised Jesus up in three days (healed) so, of course, it can be done, but for the most of us this season takes a while. Maturity is also a part of being in a season. We need to grow up in our season to get to the next one. If we do not grow from what happened, our wounds remain open and can cause a relapse, leading to more damage both spiritually and physically. All of the things we need for healing are in the season that God places us in at any one time. Then, when we move into the next season, everything is already there waiting for us. God is never caught off guard—He is the perfect planner. We do not give Him enough credit.

> Who his own self bare our sins in his own body on the tree, that we, being dead to sins, should live unto righteousness: by whose stripes ye were healed. (1 Peter 2:24)

This season is very special; it is one in which you can really feel the closeness of God. Applied healing is a touch of love. The entire process with Christ is all about love. Because God loved us, He gave us His only Son to die for us and be healed at the same time. When we look at the reason behind life-impacting events, the entire infrastructure is built on love. To me, in this season, you can see more of God's tender loving care for us. This is a season of reflection because we tend to analyze more about the hurt, pain or brokenness. The time to heal is needed for restoration. Forgiveness is a true focus point in this season too, especially in the natural. When someone or something applies hurt, it can feel like a spear through your heart. Some have expressed that it is like a movie that plays over and over in your mind. This is a repeated process designed to keep you in the hurting phase. Only through God can the healing come forth so you can move on. A time to heal has been set aside just for you. Let go and let God mend and restore your strength as only He can do.

A time to heal season shapes us back into a healthy state to continue our journeys. I think it is pretty amazing how God designed all types of seasons just so that we could experience Him in each one of them. His timeline is fascinating because no one can measure any season. At any given time, multiple people can be experiencing the same season but the beginning and end dates will differ; nonetheless, God knows every single moment. Our Father in heaven, the Creator of time, is so mind-blowing.

An important earmark regarding this season is that we all need to respect each other's season. We all have a different footprint in life. Therefore, our walk and seasons are designed just for us. If there is someone in a healing season, our position is to pray and encourage them. Everything we go through in life is not just for our present time, but for later as well.

A Time to Break Down

A season to break down is one of impact because it involves the hand of God. When God breaks something down, it is for a divine purpose. The meaning of the word has a few definitions: "to divide into parts, to separate—intransitive verb; to stop functioning, to become inoperative, to fail in strength." [13] The Hebrew word for breakdown is parats (paw-rats), which also means "to break out." [14]

In the Old Testament, some of the things that God broke down were towers, walls, altars, and most of all stone images. In most of those cases, it was a result of sin against God. He does nothing without reason. In looking at the prophet Ezekiel in chapter 26, we can see that there was a prophecy (warning) of a serious breakdown before the act. God spoke to the prophet and told him that the Lord God was against Tyrus (Tyre in some translations) because of what was said against Jerusalem and God.

> And they shall destroy the walls of Tyrus, and breakdown her towers: I will also scrape her dust from her, and make her like the top of a rock. (Ezekiel 26:4)

> And he shall set engines of war against thy walls, and with his axes he shall break down thy towers. (Ezekiel 26:9)

> And they shall make a spoil of thy riches, and make a prey of thy merchandise: and they shall break down thy walls, and destroy thy pleasant houses: and they

shall lay thy stones and thy timber and thy dust in the midst of the water. (Ezekiel 26:12)

A little history behind Tyre: it was known for being a very prosperous trading city—well established with beautiful strong walls by the sea, where the trade ships with merchandise came in. It was also known for manufacturing specialty wood (Ezekiel 27). I am sure this was a very nice place to work with all the bells and whistles of comfort. Because it was a trading city, I'm sure there was a lot of money involved in the businesses, and I envision this workplace to be one of the giants in the working world. However, in all their riches, they became a workplace that was full of pride. Although this was history, we see history repeating itself. Today companies become rich and powerful and at times they become so big that it opens doors for pride to enter; and as a result, they assume they are untouchable. In this case, God sent a strong reminder to the people of Tyre that they were humans and not gods. We are not above Him:

> Thus saith the Lord God; Because thine heart is lifted up, and thou hast said, I am a God, I sit in the seat of God, in the midst of the seas; yet thou art a man, and not God, though thou set thine heart as the heart of God. (Ezekiel 28:2)

I think we all have seen some great businesses like Tyre that have experienced a break down. When workplaces like this are broken down, they fall like timber. Sometimes it is over long periods of time, and, in other cases, it happens quickly. I believe that this is one of the shorter seasons. A breakdown causes the operation to cease. Something that is broken down comes apart from its structure. That structure is not always tangible; intangible structures (spiritual) fall apart from the inside first. When God breaks something down, it makes a statement, and that statement brings God to the forefront—the light of knowing that God is the one who brought it down.

To break down something as large as a city can only be done by the All-Powerful God Himself. So imagine what God can break down in smaller structures. Size does not matter to God. He can break down global companies or the small independent workplace when it comes to sin. What matters to God is righteousness. Pride is a deadly sin. This was why Lucifer was kicked out of heaven. God takes this very seriously! When you see pride appear in the workplace, start praying and look out because a fall is coming. There is only one God (Jehovah). When God is with you, who can be against you? But when God is against you, no one can help you. You have to get it right with God.

Now, the prophet Jeremiah was also used instrumentally by God regarding breaking down. His assignment was outlined in Jeremiah 1:10:

> See, I have this day set thee over the nations and over the kingdoms, to root out, and to pull down, and to destroy, and to throw down, to build, and to plant. (Jeremiah 1:10)

Again, we see that some seasons are grouped together. In the scripture below, God told Jeremiah that what he had built, He would break down and likewise with plucking up what He planted.

> Thus shalt thou say unto him, The Lord saith thus; Behold, that which I have built will I break down, and that which I have planted I will pluck up, even this whole land. (Jeremiah 45:4)

God does nothing without purpose. He is all about the truth of a matter. It seems like He breaks down things that are not easily removed by man alone. Walls, towers, and altars are not readily movable structures. Walls and towers are generally used for protection, like the wall around the city. They are built to be well fortified. Historically, stones were used to build them, and when a wall was taken down, it is usually demolished. If the enemy could get past the wall of a city, they could conquer it.

The breakdown of altars is also referenced as a time when God performed an act against sin. The altar has a significant meaning; the Hebrew word is mizbeach, which refers to a raised place where sacrifices are made.[15] God is very particular about sacrifices (offerings). When God wants to know the mind of your spirit, He looks at your heart (Romans 8:27). When our hearts become deceitful, false, or divided from Him, it becomes a concern. As seen earlier with Cain and Abel, we cannot offer God just anything from our heart.

Hosea marks a situation that happened in what can be considered a workplace. During a particular time, Israel produced a lot of fruit in their land. They became very prosperous and they made some bad choices. Israel allowed the abundance of riches divide their hearts from God by building more altars. The more the land produced, the more they created sacred pillars (stone images) unto false gods. These acts were purposed in their hearts because their focus changed toward righteousness in God. Riches and wealth have a way of changing our focus, and therefore, our intent changes.

> Their heart is divided; now shall they be found faulty: he shall break down their altars, he shall spoil their images. (Hosea 10:2)

Because of the iniquity in the heart of Israel, the penalty was to visit their sins and break down their altars. Some people cannot handle prosperity—it changes their view. Many workplaces or businesses have symbolically built altars. They invest into and give offerings to the idols or others gods. Leaders or decision makers in the workplace should seek godly wisdom as to who or what they give their multiplied fruit. So many times, they forget who gave them the land to produce their fruit. Once the heart is divided from God, it opens the door for the season of breaking down of altars. In today's working world, we hear of companies being shut down, and we may or may not know the full story behind the scenes, but we do know that God's vine is not empty. Poor choices about how we handle God's fruit can invoke a season that we have to endure. In verses 12 and 13, some instructions come forth with the reason for the season:

> Sow to yourselves in righteousness, reap in mercy; break up your fallow ground: for it is time to seek the Lord, till he come and rain righteousness upon you. Ye have plowed wickedness, ye have reaped iniquity; ye have eaten the fruit of lies: because thou didst trust in thy way, in the multitude of thy mighty men. (Hosea 10:12–13)

When the breaking down season comes, usually the lesson is about loving the things of the world more than our

Father in heaven. We do not readily accept that we do this, but we do. The love of the world is a thing that creeps into our thoughts and actions until it consumes us. I do not believe that we intentionally want to sin against God, but until we remember that we have a purpose-driven life daily here on the earth, we will face many obstacles, especially in our workplaces. We cannot love the things of the world because that will override the love of the Father.

> Love not the world, neither the things that are in the world. If any man love the world, the love of the Father is not in him. (1 John 2:15)

Loving the things of the world more changes our heart because it creates another master and puts Him in the forefront. When the driver of money is purposed in your heart, you will become devoted to it—hence serving it. Your thoughts and actions become compromised with ease. This is why tithing is a challenge for some of us. The concentration on tithing places you right at the center of attention at the altar. A lot of people spend a good amount of time trying to decide if they are going to be a 100 percent tither or negotiate with ease. I am not sure whether people realize it or not, but that's the other master's touch when you engage in negotiation about what belongs to God.

In the workplace, we see a great deal of coveting when it comes to money. There can be great compromises and trade-offs in righteousness when it comes to a paycheck or raises. It is a thin line which is crossed many times.

No one can serve two masters. Either you will hate the one and love the other, or you will be devoted to the one and despise the other. You cannot serve both God and money. (Matthew 6:24 NIV)

For the love of money is the root of all evil: which while some coveted after, they have erred from the faith, and pierced themselves through with many sorrows. (1 Timothy 6:10)

I have done this before and had to repent for it. Earlier I talked about my part-time job as a waitress; I would aim to get big parties over my coworkers to obtain larger tips. I would try and change table assignments so my section would be conducive to seat larger parties of people on busy nights. The hostess and I were in the scheme together and I would give her a tip for helping me with my greed strategy. The table assignment would leave others with smaller sections with lesser opportunities for larger payouts. It wasn't long before things shifted. It seemed like the larger parties stopped coming and all the small sections were overflowing with business, therefore those section got lots of tips. God had to show me some things. He did not stop the flow of money coming into the restaurant but what He did was break down the altar I had built to multiply my fruit—the altar I had built with a divided heart. After my scheme was no longer working, God showed me something: one slow day in the restaurant, I was feeling down, but God sent one man to be a blessing to me. After I had served the man, he ended up blessing me with a very generous tip. The bill was a very small amount, but he was led to bless me with $100 tip. God used one person to bless me without me needing to chase money or scheme to get it. He showed me how He can use anybody to bless his people. We just need to have a heart and mind clean and far away from wickedness. He likes to multiply our fruit especially when we are not expecting it.

A Time to Build Up

The appointed time to build up is a positive period and could be considered as a season of encouragement because God is developing His plan. This season sometimes follows the season we just covered. God is sovereign and there may be times when He will break down something (destroy it) and it may not ever be built up again. Then there are other times when He will use the buildup season for restoration as an aftermath to the time to break down. Having gone through it, this special season serves as a much-appreciated timeframe.

In this season, God builds by ordering and uniting things; he is the only one who constructs His will (plans). The word for build in Hebrew is banah, and it means "to form, establish, construct or manufacture." [16]In addition, banah denotes rebuilding something that has been destroyed [by God]. In looking at the word up, it means "in or into an upright or higher position; advanced state."[17] The buildup process is normally a gradual accumulation or advancement.

Like the other seasons, "a time to build up" has a time span directed at an end goal. There are numerous reasons behind building up something or someone, and they are all unique because they have a valuable end result. From the time a person is born, they live in a season of building up. The breath of every human being is the breath of God—for that reason, they are a part of His created end goal for life.

Every end goal of life points toward Christ whether a person believes in Jesus or not. The truth of the matter is, Jesus died for everyone including nonbelievers, therefore their life was created to be a part of that end goal, and no man or any religious belief can ever change that. Now, a person may forfeit their right to live in eternity in God and spend eternity in hell instead—that is totally up to the individual and is their freewill option. Nevertheless, Jesus is and will always be the way, the truth and the life to eternity. This invitation is open to all.

> Jesus saith unto him, I am the way, the truth, and the life: no man cometh unto the Father, but by me. (John 14:6)

Some may ask what the end goal of eternal life in God has to do with the workplace. Well, it has everything to do with the workplace. God is constantly building, developing and rebuilding things in our lives, especially in the workplace to help us accomplish goals—goals that have been designed for us to win in this cycle of life. If there were no goals in place, what would be the purpose of living? To have everlasting life in God is a great benefit to look forward to.

The workplace helps prepare us for that goal. It is also a good place of learning because it directs us toward moral excellence. It is full of opportunities to help us to live forever. Milestones are important markers in the development stage. While we are in a work position on earth, there are some strategic markers in our buildup season. Sometimes we hit bumps in the road (hindrances) while in the development phase and those bumps are there to see how we react to them. They can be circumstances or situations that have a direct impact on our integrity and character.

God grooms us (builds us up) to be of good character so He can use us for His glory. The workplace is always good testing ground for building us up. Whenever there is testing going on in your life, the enemy will be larking around too. The enemy likes hanging out at the workplace so He can present options to damage your character and compromise your integrity as a child of God. Developing the good in our lives requires good character. A time to build up is a repeatable season because we never arrive at that place of perfection. As long as we live here on earth, there will be new development and growth processes, both of which help build up our character and integrity.

This season prepares us for what is to come. When a building is finished being built, it is ready to be occupied for a purpose. Once God builds us up we are ready for the assigned purpose. If our character is not ready for the assignment, it can derail and lead us off course. Keep in mind this refers to us being in the will of God.

We cannot expect the blessing of God to flow in our lives if we are lying, cheating or stealing. The fruit of those characteristics brings heartache and pain as a result of deceit. Some view this as a small issue because it is so widely spread within God's people. When God builds up the walls in your life, He will address anything that does not represent Him, which will, therefore, need to be corrected in order to build up character. Clearly, the three examples given do not represent the life Christ lived. Being that he is still our example, here are some thoughts on each one of these character building impediments:

Lying—This character breaker is a serious offense because it is full-blown deception. Everything our Father in heaven is established on is truth. Everything about Him is just, pure and true. You cannot bend the truth—it stands forever. A lie is breakable because it is only a reflection of truth. It is so important that we practice the principal of truth in our daily walk. There is no such thing as a small or white lie—all lies are harmful.

In the workplace, there is no room for lies because it is a trigger to activate other evil acts. So, why not tell the truth? The only one ashamed of truth is the devil, who is the father of all lies. A liar is considered a child of the devil, but I say nullify that relationship and speak the truth no matter what.

> Ye are of your father the devil, and the lusts of your father ye will do. He was a murderer from the beginning, and abode not in the truth, because there is no truth in him. When he speaketh a lie, he speaketh of his own: for he is a liar, and the father of it. (John 8:44)

Cheating—A cheater is unprincipled, and promotes dishonesty. Someone who cheats is not wise because cheating can never be hidden. When you cheat someone out of something that usually belongs to them, who are you really betraying? What is rarely recognized, especially in the workplace, is their act is never done in secret. God sees all, and there is nothing hidden from Him. Just as a cheater is double-crossing, their reaping is multiplied in consequences. To this point, cheating never really wins. A cheater's measurements are off, and a cheater always assumes victory, but the truth is, in reality, they lose because the consequences are always greater.

Acts 5 talks about the story of Ananias and Sapphira whom cheated with their giving of profits made from selling their land. At this time, anyone who sold their house or land gave the increase to the apostles who in return gave gifts to those in need. The people were one in heart and mind in that workplace, and they loved and shared with one another. Ananias brought only a portion of the profits to Apostle Peter. A cheater assumes they fool others; in this case, Peter was not fooled, as the Holy Spirit revealed the deception. As a consequence, Ananias dropped down and died right there. Then his wife Sapphira came to where they were and proclaimed the same dishonest amount: long story short, she fell down also and died at Peter's feet. I know this sounds very extreme, but it is a true story with a hard point to be made. When we attempt to cheat others, we must realize that we are attempting to cheat God. All things belong to Him; we are just managers over the things we have for a little while. As God is building us up, we learn more of the good than bad—let's choose to do good!

> Therefore to him that knoweth to do good, and doeth it not, to him it is sin. (James 4:17)

Stealing—Stealing is taking without consent, and is often driven by covetousness, lust, addiction, or an inner yearn. For more clarity on this habit-forming characteristic, it can also be considered as robbery, embezzlement, misappropriation, abduction, carjacking, kidnapping, or even black marketeering, and so on. When taking someone's property wrongfully, it is a trespass not only against the person but against God also. Some may not want to view it as such, but until we understand the powerful profile of God, then we will remain in an ignorant state. We were born into this world with nothing, therefore we own nothing, which is why we cannot take anything with us when we die.

There are huge consequences for this act in the workplace. There is no little act of stealing: taking office supplies, including ink pens, is an offense to God. Stealing time to receive pay for hours not worked is an offense against God also. When you are in leadership and an employee has earned a raise and you don't apply your effort to see that they receive it, you are stealing the opportunity for their advancement. When companies underpay their employees because of their personal greed, that is also stealing what rightfully belongs to others that have performed the work. When you overcharge for services or products, you are stealing in the eyes of God. If more businesses evaluated their pay structures periodically for fairness and righteousness, they would have an overflow of blessings that they would not have room enough to receive.

Now, many of them may focus on the charitable part of giving, but they miss this important part: he Bible says in Genesis 12:3, when He spoke to Abraham, that He would bless those that bless you. When businesses begin to focus on blessing God's people verses stealing from them, it makes room for God to bless that business.

> You shall not steal; you shall not deal falsely; neither lie one to another. (Leviticus 19:11)

There are a lot of things that hinder the work God is trying to develop within us during the buildup season; those above are just a few. Nevertheless, we are all a work in progress, but check points in our life help save us from being over-processed in certain seasons. The reason God builds us up is so we can excel in every area of our lives. The workplace is a seasonal place that gives us that opportunity to excel.

Another reference to this season is the continuous goal of building up the church. This is a specific time span (church age) which serves between Jesus death and his second coming. We as believers are still pressing toward this mark. Jesus made a life-changing statement that set the foundations of our faith. As believers, we are still building on that same foundation mentioned in Matthew 16:18: "You are Peter, and upon this rock I will build my church." There are a couple of key words in this scripture that conjoin the true meaning of what the church should be built on:

> Peter (Petros in Greek, means "a piece of rock" [18]) was a disciple/apostle (leader) who made a confession that Jesus was the Christ. He represents leadership, which is a piece of the rock that helps to build up the church.
>
> Rock (Petra in Greek, means "mass of rock; detached stone or boulder" [19]): this solid rock represents Jesus and his unmovable works. The church must have a solid foundation to build upon. Peter's confession about who Jesus is vitally important because it gives us that foundation. He is our rock and cornerstone of our faith.
>
> Church (Ekklesia in Greek, means "a calling out; a group of people called out for a special purpose"[20]). Jesus is the founder of the church, which consists of a company (body) of proclaimed believers. Until Jesus comes back for his glorious Church, we must continue to build up.

4: A time to weep, and a time to laugh; a time to mourn, and a time to dance;

A Time to Weep

This season we all know too well. This is one of the first passionate expressions we experience when we are born from the womb. To weep is to demonstrate an outward expression of how we are feeling. Weeping is often times related to mourning, which is also another season mentioned in Ecclesiastes 3. The Bible first mention of the weep is when Abraham wept for Sarah in her passing (Genesis 23:2), then again it is mentioned after Jacob kissed Rachael (Genesis 29:11). So we see that a time to weep is referenced as two distinct forms: (1) to weep in sorrow, and (2) in joy. Nevertheless, both are shedding of tears.

The Hebrew translation is bakah (baw-kaw), simply meaning "to weep, bewail, cry or shed tears." [21] The Greek translation is klaio (klah`-os), also used as a loud expression in an audible form.[22] Both translations are referenced often as a formal expression of grief, with sounds like groaning.

The workplace can hold many narratives that have impacted our lives, and those sequence of events have caused us to weep at times. Two important reminders before we continue:

1. We all have a workplace on the earth that holds an assignment directed with a purpose, driven by a process.
2. A season refers to an appointed time in God.

There is an appointed time to weep. Although weeping can be an outward expression, many of us weep silently over situations and circumstances that we have experienced in our workplaces. To weep is a natural articulation because it is a pressing out of our heart. Even Jesus wept because of the love in his heart. Only God can create us to react to both joy and pain with one shared trait—to weep.

Even though we endure weeping at times for various reasons, there were some instances when Jesus said to weep not, because of his compassion for us. He experienced compassion just as we do. In some cases, the words weep not can be an assertion to comfort and lean on faith because God's work is to follow:

> And when the Lord saw her, he had compassion on her, and said unto her, Weep not....And he said, Young man, I say unto thee, Arise. And he that was dead sat up, and began to speak. (Luke 7:13–15)

> And all wept, and bewailed her: but he said, Weep not; she is not dead, but sleepeth. And they laughed him to scorn, knowing that she was dead. And he put them all out, and took her by the hand, and called, saying, Maid, arise. And her spirit came again, and she arose straightway. (Luke 11:52–54)

The works of Christ are always shown in love despite of what we see or feel in the natural. Grief is one of those heartfelt emotions that, we can all agree, it is hard not to weep over; yet in the scripture above, that is what Jesus was stating. In that moment, you have to admit this would be a hard thing to do, but what he is trying to get us to see is that the weeping season is a temporary process. The work that happens behind the scenes is much greater.

Psalms 30:5 beautifully describes how God's favor is life. All that Jesus did while here on the earth was to point to life. When we can embrace this, then we know that joy follows the weeping.

> For his anger endureth but a moment; in his favour is life: weeping may endure for a night, but joy cometh in the morning. (Psalm 30:5)

It takes faith to believe that no matter what adversity we face, especially in the workplace, there is joy in the end. I've learned that faith is so powerful. It seems easy when said, but it can be very hard at times. Faith is surrounded by work. Through faith, the work gets done. It is named as one of the power gifts of the Holy Spirit. For a long time, I did not view faith as a power gift, but the more God revealed Himself through faith, the more I was strengthened with the power of faith. It takes great faith to conquer grief, sorrow, pain, anger, hurt, disappointment, and other attributes that cause weeping. But it is imperative that we exercise the power of our faith in God in this season.

> But though he cause grief, yet will he have compassion according to the multitude of his mercies. For he doth not afflict willingly nor grieve the children of men. (Lamentations 3:32–33)

Some years back, I worked for a large firm whose aim was to be a global empire in their industry. The company was growing successfully at a very fast pace, but it seemed like during the climb to the top, some core values were becoming diluted. The company's caring focus on the wellbeing of its customers and employees changed a bit. The race to the top was exciting and they had more work than they could handle in some areas of the company; their company stock was doing very well, and their image was being polished. One day I came to work to learn that a group of us was being outsourced to another company that owned the systems but would still perform some of the same job functions. I was not happy about this change and did not understand why this was only happening to our department. Without any say in the matter, we had to adjust to a new structure of work. I was angry and disappointed about the change, and I wept about it because the change was a sphere in my life. I measured my success by who I worked for...or so I thought.

The new way of performing my job changed drastically, and I found myself discouraged and I felt mad most days about my seasonal process in the workplace. This new company was much smaller, and I could not see the benefit of me working for them. But God worked through my pain—I had to learn new concepts, methodologies and, most of all, I had to produce multiple forms of writing. There were times I wrote so much that I had dreams of writing. I did not realize it then, but God was setting me up for my purpose. We cannot see the work that God is doing behind the scenes; we forget that the master planner and time keeper of life is working things out for our good for those who love Him and called according to His purpose (Romans 8:28).

After being acclimated to the job for some time, the company that I desired to remain working for took a downward spiral that impacted their company status and a lot of the employees: God had seen what I could not! In addition, there was a greater benefit to my work process when He planted me in the other company. This company prepared me for the work that I am doing right now. My season to weep was over, and joy came to give me a greater outlook on my future.

All seasons are important, but I feel that the ones we overlook the most have a lasting impact on our growth and our journey in life. There is nothing we can do to stop the season to weep, but we can choose to interrupt it if we use the power of faith to trust that God is working things out for our good.

The prophet Jeremiah has an encouraging message concerning weeping. Remember there is a reward at the end for the one who weeps.

> Thus saith the Lord; Refrain thy voice from weeping, and thine eyes from tears: for thy work shall be rewarded, saith the Lord; (Jeremiah 31:16)

A Time to Laugh

There is a time to laugh, and this is not only admired but considered healthy. Some believe that laughter reduces pain, and helps the heart. When we laugh, there is a sense of cheer in our heart. The Bible tells us that a merry heart does well like medicine (Proverbs 17:22), and is, therefore, a form of healing. In the workplace, this is a much-needed virtue.

Laughter has a way of shifting an environment. Many times, when we are working under pressure in a stressful working environment, the stress opens the door for other negative forces to enter. The timing of laughter is key just like any other appointed season. Remember a season is not on a man-measured time clock.

Merriam-Webster gives a definition of laugh as to show emotion of joy or pleasure in something[23]. This is a positive, but on the other hand laughter can be an expression of scorn, mockery or disrespect, thus creating a negative vibe. Laughter is an outward expression, but we should be mindful of the source behind the laughter. Our countenance can sometimes display the meaning behind the laugh.

The Hebrew word for laugh in this reference is sachaq (saw-khak), and it means "to laugh in pleasure, play or detraction— meaning to mock or scorn." [24]

Laughter can be a moment in time, but this season is also seen in our scriptures as a time when God laughs. Yes, the King of kings, Lord of lords, and the Alpha and Omega laughs! God is all-knowing, all-seeing of everything, and I believe that people forget the fact that nothing is hidden from Him. He sees the wicked in the world and the mockery they make of Him, so He laughs for periods of time.

> He that sitteth in the heavens shall laugh: the Lord shall have them in derision. (Psalm 2:4)

> But thou, O Lord, shalt laugh at them; thou shalt have all the heathen in derision. (Psalm 59:8)

There are times when we lose sight of who God is and what He requires of us. From the heavens He sees our every move, including in our workplace. When we mistreat or trespass against one another, God knows. He does not react quickly all the time, but instead waits for an appointed time. The scripture above shows that God laughs, but in reading chapter 2, this scripture is referring to the how the people take counsel against God and His anointed. As a result, God will have them in derision; meaning scorned, ridiculed or made a laughingstock. God always has the last laugh.

In the workplace, I have witnessed this many times. A lot of times when we are experiencing different types of adversity in the workplace, we forget that God is watching. There is one scripture I know all too well and one that should always remain at the forefront of our thoughts before we mistreat someone:

> Be not deceived; God is not mocked: for whatsoever a man soweth, that shall he also reap. (Galatians 6:7)

This is wonderful when we sow good seeds, but the reaping of the bad has a greater outcome. When God is laughing, there may be time to get it right, but when the derision comes, it is not a good seat to sit in. We do things a lot of times without knowing what the consequences will be. Every workplace has its seasons, and they change without notice. There are many who sadly assume they choose the start and finish timelines in their life; however, God has proven that we do not.

The season to laugh is not always joyful for the ones being laughed at. Just because God's hand is not moving, does not mean He is silent—perhaps He is laughing because He can see the day of change approaching. Psalms 52 below says that God will also allow the righteous to see when the tables turn so that we may fear our Holy God.

> The Lord shall laugh at him: for he seeth that his day is coming. (Psalm 37:13)

> The righteous also shall see, and fear, and shall laugh at him: (Psalm 52:6)

This season is one that carries a deeper reminder concerning laughter: just as we laugh with ease, so does God. He created us to experience laughter, joy and good cheer, but along with these, He still wants us to love one another. Our aim should be to live a righteous life at all times, especially in our workplace. When we compromise with work ethics, we must remember it separates us from God.

A Time to Mourn

To mourn is a season that we do not look forward to. This is a time when we experience grief and sorrow. Mourning comes without a specific time allotted to endure it. In this time, there is great sadness about something that has occurred in our life. A time to mourn can be a result of someone's death, or it could be the absence or loss of something/someone that has been removed from our presence.

Life experiences in the workplace can become shared events with people we are involved with on a daily basis. There are times when we disclose our griefs and cares with one another in an attempt for comfort. God is fully aware of everything we are dealing with in life. This scripture is a reminder that God can remove the desire of our eyes—that which becomes the sorrow of our hearts. When this happens, we enter into a time of mourning. God is not a respecter of persons; therefore, no one is exempt from this season.

> Then Peter opened his mouth, and said, Of a truth I perceive that God is no respecter of persons. (Acts 10:34)

Another strong point is we all belong to God, and if we are blessed enough to have someone in our lives, it is because He granted it. These can be life comforters but God removes them as He pleases. We have to accept this. So, when the time to mourn comes, we should remain as strong as we possibly can.

When we mourn life-changing events, the mourning process is very different from the initial loss of a loved one. Both are filled with sorrow, but the dimension of grief is greater. I believe the season has a longer lifespan.

There is a very interesting but heartfelt narrative in the book of Ezekiel, chapter 24:15–27, in which it talks about the death of Ezekiel's wife. God instructed him not to mourn. When someone as close as a wife dies, it is only natural to mourn. I realize that Ezekiel was a powerful prophet, but he is not exempt from our natural ability to mourn due to the loss of a loved one.

God spoke to Ezekiel beforehand and told him that He was going to take the delight of his eyes (his wife) away from him at a stroke; yet Ezekiel was not to mourn or weep, neither should he shed a tear. Now, he could sigh but not out loud, and in addition, Ezekiel could not show any mourning for the dead. He also told him to "bind his turban, put his shoes on; do not cover your lips, nor eat the bread of men." Now, this had to be a lot to swallow. The things of God are not always easy to comprehend in the natural—even with some spiritual understanding, it is still hard: God thinks beyond what we can imagine. And Ezekiel had to be a strong man of God to carry out this assignment, just to prove that God's word is true. Verse 18 says that he spoke to the people in the morning, and his wife died that evening. The next morning, he carried out the instructions from God. Although this was a time to mourn because of the loss of his wife, God's assignment was greater.

Side bar: Ezekiel was in his workplace; the house of Israel worked together.

The people asked Ezekiel what was the meaning behind all of this. So, he enlightened them with God's message of how when these things happen to them; they were also instructed not to mourn:

> Then I answered them, The word of the Lord came unto me, saying, Speak unto the house of Israel, Thus saith the Lord God; Behold, I will profane my sanctuary, the excellency of your strength, the desire of your eyes, and that which your soul pitieth; and your sons and your daughters whom ye have left shall fall by the sword. And ye shall do as I have done: ye shall not cover your lips, nor eat the bread of men. And your tires shall be upon your heads, and your shoes upon your feet: ye shall not mourn nor weep; but ye shall pine away for your iniquities, and mourn one toward another. Thus Ezekiel is unto you a sign: according to all that he hath done

shall ye do: and when this cometh, ye shall know that I am the Lord God. (Ezekiel 24:20–24)

The message in this is harsh, as God uses the things we experience in life for our lessons. Some are unbearable and unreal because of tragic afflictions that God allows. Our God is loving, caring and sincere when it comes to righteousness. He sacrificed His Son so that we could live, yet many still do not give God a whisper of thanks. Our hearts ache for the loss of someone we love deeply, but we never stop to think about what it really costs for us to live. Our jobs are merely the size of a rain drop in the bucket of how God really wants to bless us. Many of us take people for granted in our workplaces. The mistreatment and trespasses we inflict upon one another are not what God wants when He assigns us to work together in brotherly love.

At the end of the scripture, it gives us the reason for God's action: so they will know that I am the Lord. Now, this is the house of Israel that Ezekiel is speaking to, and I am sure they have heard of the name of the Lord, but for God to respond with this message, He is implying that they "do not know him!"; not knowing Him in a sense of not fearing who He is. Evidently their lifestyles or actions were not a reflection of the image that God made us in. When we rebel against God, it does not go unpunished, even in "grace." We can be forgiving because Jesus died for us, and we can have everlasting life, but God is still our heavenly Father. He did not send His only begotten Son for our redemption so that we can live anyway we want to and still get all of the great benefits of everlasting life.

Although Ezekiel could not show his emotions for the loss of his wife outwardly, I believe he still mourned inwardly. Mourning is a state of being as a result of hurt or pain, and it is internal. It happens on the inside where the deepness of our hearts beat and no one except God can actually know the sensitivity of the pain. A time to mourn is a season that puts us in touch with the pain that Christ endured for us. He died for each one of us; therefore, all of us will share in that season of mourning. As days come and go, we all become acquainted with the removal of our comforts and of those we love, and we all experience a time to mourn.

A Time to Dance

The definition of the dance is to move or move up and down or about in a lively manner; [25]sometimes to attend in a zealous and servile manner; a series of rhythmic and patterned bodily movements usually performed to music. I really had to rely on the Holy Spirit to minister to me regarding this season. Although the obvious dance is in a form of cheer, the reasoning behind the dance may not be. Again, God allows these seasons because it is a part of the process and He knows what is to come afterward.

This appointed time, referenced in Ecclesiastes, points to when the wicked dance for a season: in that season, they rejoice in their current status or in their way of living. The Hebrew word for dance is raqad (raw-kad), meaning "to skip about, leap wildly or for joy."[26] We should all be familiar with dancing with joy and with dancing in a wild way. To be clear, dance is not evil, but the dancing as a result of something evil makes the dance immoral. There are two other scriptures that reference this form of the word dance: Job 21:11 and Isiah 13:21.

Job speaks about how they sent forth their little ones like a flock (numerous) and their children danced. The focus here is knowing that the "they" refers to the wicked and "their" refers to the children of the wicked. When a wicked lifestyle is being reflected by parents, in most cases, the children adopt the same lifestyle. We are the daily coaches entrusted by God who made us parents over our children, and we have a hand in establishing the environment they live in. We can promote them to do evil, or encourage them to do well in the eyes of God.

Job speaks of this because the wicked have included their children in acts of evil as a reflection of them. The child is a heritage of the Lord and considered a reward of the womb (Psalms 127:3); yet "they" send their children to partake in this season to dance also. This is a great reminder of how we should be training our children in the correct way to go, so that when they are old, they will not depart from their path—words of wisdom by King Solomon. Our aim is to teach our children to live a righteous life no matter how much the parents fall short. There is grace and mercy through Christ, but God's word is very clear about living a righteous life; and Job warns that the unrighteous will drink the wrath of God.

> Wherefore do the wicked live, become old, yea, are mighty in power? Their seed is established in their sight with them, and their offspring before their eyes. ... They send forth their little ones like a flock, and their children dance. They take the timbrel and harp, and rejoice at the sound of the organ. They spend their days in wealth, and in a moment go down to the grave. (Job 21:7–13)

> God layeth up his iniquity for his children: he rewardeth him, and he shall know it. His eyes shall see his destruction, and he shall drink of the wrath of the Almighty. (Job 21:19–20)

When evil or ill intent is the foundation of your celebration, you have entered into a season and have welcomed the opportunity for the wrath of God to come upon you. When I was younger, there was a quote we use to say: "The same that make you laugh will make you cry." At times I found these words to be true; unbeknownst to me at that time, they were seasons that were written in the Bible. You laugh at something one minute, and it could be the very thing that makes you cry at a later time.

Personally, I cannot relate to what makes evil doers laugh and rejoice at the pain or hurt of others. Also, I have seen this on many occasions in the workplace: belittling, laughing and making fun at those that may not have educational backgrounds or the same opportunities as others, or are unlike others because they have been created differently by God. These types of prejudices are also imparted to children. Jesus endured this all too well while he was being taken to the cross. He was the righteous-one and yet "they" spat on him, made a mockery of him, and rejoiced at him being chastised until death. I wonder how many of their children watched or even participated in that evil act or season.

The prophet Isaiah writes about the day of the Lord and the destruction of Babylon (empire/kingdom) by Almighty God, and about how He will punish the world for its evil (Isaiah 13). Isaiah describes it as a day when all hands will be faint and all men's heart will melt. Men and women will experience fear and pain when the Destroyer (God) lays their land desolate, and the sinners will be destroyed. In Isaiah 13:21, it says that "the satyrs shall dance there," meaning that the place referred to shall become a desolate waste. [27]

> But wild beasts of the desert shall lie there; and their houses shall be full of doleful creatures; and owls shall dwell there, and satyrs shall dance there. (Isaiah 13:21)

The satyr is referred in Greek mythology as a beast (devil) composed of a man and a goat,[28] alleged to occupy uninhabited and desolate territories. The Vulgate renders its meaning to them as; Beasts, demons, or dragons. They danced frequently in the ruins of the desolate city (Babylon.) It is believed that these beasts would dance on certain nights called the "night of life" in honor of Satan. Does the term nightlife sound familiar? Is that not where many of us perform most of our dances—in the night hours?

When someone dances, they are reacting evidently to what they believe in, whether the cause or occasion for dance is for good or evil. God created us to have movement in our body and to respond as we choose. The reflection of our dance is an outward response to what we take in. Our hearing is internal, and when we respond to music being heard internally, our body can easily respond by making a movement outwardly. We just need to be careful as to what our bodily movements are responding to.

King David was known to dance unto the Lord. Spiritual movement is important because the true intent of dance is to be done unto the Lord in spirit and truth. When we respond to worship outwardly in praise or heartfelt worship, it is pleasing unto the Lord God. Godly music is intended for us to rejoice at the sound and respond to God in adoration and gratification. Satan was a worshipper before he was kicked out of heaven, so I am not surprised that he has devil worshippers dancing for him—he is such a counterfeiter and yearns for people to worship him. Worldly music and dance was inspired by Satan to lure us away from authentic holy worship unto God. Some may not want to accept this, but the teaching on the foundations of worship and spiritual dance is a deeper lesson that is covered in vast writings by other authors. I encourage you to take a deeper dive into this study for more understanding.

A time to dance is unique because it enlightens us that God watches every movement we make to define the source of our actions. He sees our hearts from afar, and He knows our thoughts behind our movements even in the workplace.

Sometimes we can view God as a strong pillar—one who can destroy anything by his touch. Then, He is that soft spoken one in the still of the day who whispers creations by the sound of His words, and the movement of His power upon the earth. The Almighty is befitting unto our God. A time to dance can launch you into a spiritual experience of worship with God, or it can open access doors to be evil. Choose your dance wisely.

5: A time to cast away stones, and a time to gather stones together; a time to embrace, and a time to refrain from embracing;

A Time to Cast Away Stones

A time to cast away stones is a season also referred to as to scatter stones, which is translated in the New International Version of the Bible. To scatter means to cause to separate widely; it can also indicate a force or power that drives things or people to separate in many directions. [29]Other translations, such as the amplified, say to throw away stones.

The word stone in Hebrew is eben (eh`-ben), from the root of banah, through the meaning "to build; a stone."[30] Referred to as a building material: well covers, tablets, sling-stones, altars, and memorials are made of stone. Eben is most exclusively used for movable stone(s).

There is a time to cast away stones, and it is part of removing something that was previously built. This is a clearing out process to prepare for what is to come forth. Stones are used for memorials to mark something of the past as a reminder. This could have a two-fold effect: it can be a positive to serve for sentimental value for a period of time; but on the other hand, it can be a negative, because if stones are in place, they can become a stumbling block for building up the future. If we hold onto the things of the past, we cannot move forward in the things that God has for us. To cast away stones is to move them out of the way. This is not to say we cannot reuse them to rebuild something new, but there is a time to cast them away. Stones are precious and useful for building strong, solid foundations, so we need them, but we need to know when to let them go too. At times, we hold on to the things that God is trying to get us to release. Stones can be symbolic of things that are strong and rugged in our lives. Some stones can block our path so we cannot get to our destination. Psalms 91 speaks of the Angel baring us up in their hands lest we dash our foot against the stone. We can relate how it feels to dash/smash our foot on a rock—it hurts, and then we want to cast the stone away. But if we remove them when it is time, we can avoid some unforeseen pain.

Some stones were formed years ago, and over time they start to crumble, but although we want to hold on to what is familiar, we dare to make room for the new and improved stone that God wants to give to us. In our workplaces, we build up our positions with stones of belief that we will remain there for extended periods of time. We build our own types of altars, well covers (private workspaces), our own writing in stone, all as if we are going to be there forever; then we wonder why our foot keeps hitting against the stone and causing us pain.

It is amazing how we will keep stones in our path and create ways to get around them rather than casting them away. One of my workplace assignments was for a specialty insurance company. Their daily operations were comprised of large company initiatives. The corporate company was very prosperous and seemed to treat their employees well, and I was excited to work with a large team of people, learning new aspects about the business with plans to be there for a long time. The project was estimated to last a couple of years.

After about six months, our entire department was called into a meeting, and we were told by executives that the company had decided to pull the plug on the project I was working on and invest in another project instead. The room went silent, as we were all informed that this would be the end of our jobs. I could not believe that after investing major funds in the project, they would change lanes at the drop of a hat. In retrospect, this company had specific goals—to win at all costs. They were a publicly traded company, and they did what was best for the company, not for the employees. This works for some, but not for all. I was grasping, trying to hold on to every stone I could by applying for other jobs, just trying to stay afloat; but that stone was sinking fast. Finally, I realized it was time to let go. God always has a plan, and once I moved the stone out of my way, He was able to bless me with another assignment. When it is time to cast away the stone, trust God and let it go.

Another interesting fact about the stone is that in biblical days, if there was a sign of human leprosy (plague) in a household and suspicious spots appeared on a stone, the stone was required to be removed from its structure and cast away, as the stones were considered unclean as well (Leviticus 14). When a stone is attached to something that is considered evil, it must be removed to avoid continuous spreading.

Although this points to the law in the Old Testament pertaining to being unclean, it can also be considered symbolic of removing anything that is attached to sin, which maps to the New Testament. God's word continues to map back to every area of our lives, and He uses simple things such as a stone to teach us about seasons. How often do we walk past stones or rocks in the road and view them as little value? But our omnipotent God values everything in creation. This season of is obviously very important to God else it would not be called out as an appointed time.

> But God hath chosen the foolish things of the world to confound the wise; and God hath chosen the weak things of the world to confound the things which are mighty; (1 Corinthians 1:27)

A Time to Gather Stones

The opposite of casting away stones is to gather them. Gathering of stones is a working season. When we view the gathering of something as unique as the stone, it must have a significant meaning. This is a season of great purpose because it is attached to a greater plan.

The Hebrew word gather in this context is kanac (kaw-nas), meaning "to collect; hence, to enfold, gather together, heap up." [31]

To gather stones is not to keep but to use for a purpose. This season is solely preparation for another season. This is a season of wisdom. The book of Proverbs speaks of the ant and how her ways of gathering for a season are wise. She even uses the rocks/stones to build her home.

> Go to the ant, thou sluggard; consider her ways, and be wise: Which having no guide, overseer, or ruler, provideth her meat in the summer, and gathereth her food in the harvest. (Proverbs 6:6–8)

The ants are a people not strong, yet they prepare their meat in the summer;

> The conies are but a feeble folk, yet make they their houses in the rocks; (Proverbs 30:25–26)

To gather stones during an appointed time is to plan for a harvest. That harvest may or may not be for the person actually gathering. We are all a part of a greater plan; all of us make up God's divine plan. As we walk through life, we have been chosen to pick up and gather things to build for God's glory. Only a self-centered person would think that everything they gather is for them. It does not matter if we plan to save what we are gathering for ourselves—God can still use it whenever He wants to. He can turn the hearts of kings if he wants to and cause them to give it away at any given moment— you know how hard a king's heart can be.

> The king's heart is in the hand of the Lord, as the rivers of water: he turneth it whithersoever he will. (Proverbs 21:1)

Both King David and King Solomon understood all too well about gathering together stones. It was laid on their hearts to build the temple, and over a period of time, they gathered what was needed to build the temple. What is really amazing is, although it took an extreme amount of the best materials to build the temple, there was more than enough wealth to live off. When we gather stones for the glory of God, it is an opportunity for Him to multiply what we have left.

In the gathering of stone season, while preparing to build the temple, King David even gave orders to the foreigners in Israel and appointed stonecutters of them to prepare the stones for the building project. He was focused on the purpose, and he stretched beyond the Israelites to fulfill the purpose. In these seasons that God allows, we should make each one count by seizing every opportunity within our reach.

> And David commanded to gather together the strangers that were in the land of Israel; and he set masons to hew wrought stones to build the house of God. (1 Chronicles 22:2)

While we are in our workplaces, there will be times when we are to gather stones only. Our periods of gathering stones are repeated processes because the sole purpose is to gather. This is not the season to build but to prepare to build. This particular timeline may seem like you are running on a treadmill, going nowhere. The gathering process is not an exciting time, because you may not be doing anything new. Week after week, month after month, and maybe even year after year and nothing has changed in your process—it is because you are simply in a season to gather stones. This process is an exercise in remaining steadfast as you evolve in purpose. It is a mind-set challenge for endurance, self-control, and strength of will. Be obedient and try hard not to complain; most of all try not to rush the season out. Wait and continue to collect your stones until God changes your season. What He is using you to build will be a blessing to many, as this season is essential to His plan.

A Time to Embrace

To embrace means to clasp, hold, grasp or hug; to take up especially readily or gladly. You can embrace someone or something; to take in or include as part, item, or element of a more inclusive whole, as stated by Merriam-Webster.[32] The Hebrew word chabaq (khaw-bak) carries the same meaning: "to clasp; to fold one's hands in idleness." [33]

Embracing can be hugging or holding someone closely to articulate love or friendship. This is seen a lot of times in marriages to suggest strong feelings. This is also seen expressively with a mother and child. I particularly like the narrative in the Bible when it talks about how Elisha wanted to show his gratitude to the Shunammite woman who demonstrated great care for the prophet and his servant by setting up a room for them to lay their head when they traveled through. The prophet Elisha prophesized to her that she would embrace a child in a season, according to the time of life. The prophet's words came to pass, and the woman bared and embraced a child in the season.

> And he said, What then is to be done for her? And Gehazi answered, Verily she hath no child, and her husband is old. And he said, Call her. And when he had called her, she stood in the door. And he said, About this season, according to the time of life, thou shalt embrace a son....And the woman conceived, and bare a son at that season that Elisha had said unto her, according to the time of life. (2 Kings 4:14–17)

This time of embracing was certainly a season according to the time of life—as in all of our seasons. God carves out these seasons within His divine will to move us to embrace our purpose-driven life as well. I love that God owns and operates a master plan that man has no power over. Just knowing that He sees the end beforehand should give us comfort in each season. We could never know the things about ourselves that God knows, which is why it is important to trust Him. I would much rather be a part of God's plan than Satan's. These seasons are jointly fitted to our lives and if we trust Him 100 percent with everything, we can live a worry-free life. No one can protect and care for you like God. When we can pause for a moment and think about how God has embraced us, it warms our hearts beyond measure. He never gets tired of unfolding our mapped-out life, season after season, just so we can know Him even the more. His aim is for us to dwell with Him forever, and each season prepares us for that goal.

A great thing we all have the ability to do is embrace wisdom. King Solomon was a man of great wisdom. In Proverbs 4, he talks about the security in having wisdom and the results of what happens if we embrace it. There are seasons to obtain wisdom. What I like about this season is we do not have to wait to get wisdom. Solomon says that wisdom is the principal thing, meaning it is fundamental. When we can understand a thing, we then chose to use sound judgment. Wisdom is knowledge, and when we embrace it, we gain more understanding.

> Get wisdom, get understanding: forget it not; neither decline from the words of my mouth. Forsake her not, and she shall preserve thee: love her, and she shall keep thee. Wisdom is the principal thing; therefore get wisdom: and with all thy getting get understanding. Exalt her, and she shall promote thee: she shall bring thee to honour, when thou dost embrace her. (Proverbs 4:5–8)

Even though we can get wisdom any time, this season is called out because there are seasons when we should spend time getting wisdom. Reading and seeking knowledge is time well spent. There are seasons when we intake godly wisdom to help us in life. The more time we spend in studying God's word, the more wisdom we acquire. Godly knowledge is the highest form of wisdom. Think about it—who has more wisdom than God? Even Satan has embraced the wisdom of the things of God; this is why he wants to be Him.

A Time to Refrain from Embracing

To refrain from something is to keep oneself from doing, touching, or indulging in something, particularly from impulse.[34] In Hebrew, refrain is translated as rachaq (raw-khak), meaning "to widen in any direction; make far; it is used to express numerous types of distance." [35]

As mentioned in the season of embracing earlier, it was indicated that embracing could refer to people being held together closely or hugging tightly. In most marriage chambers, couples embrace in this form to show their affection for one another. However, there is a time/season when couples are to refrain from embracing normally by mutual consent. The Bible speaks about these matters.

> Defraud ye not one the other, except it be with consent for a time, that ye may give yourselves to fasting and prayer; and come together again, that Satan tempt you not for your incontinency. (1 Corinthians 7:5)

There can be set times to abstain from embracing with one another in order to devote oneself to intimate time with God by fasting and praying. This time of solitude will allow them to wholly focus on God without distractions. However, within a marriage, this should not be a prolonged season as it is important for a couple to maintain their union as one flesh. This is a short season in order to avoid being tempting by the enemy with other sexual desires.

Another reference to refraining from embracing is when the Lord told Moses to go to the people and consecrate them. One of the instructions was for the men to not be intimate with a woman. Again, this is a set time to reframe from embracing with one another.

In the effort of living a consecrated life for those who are not married, in order to maintain self-control, single men and women should refrain from embracing others in ways that lead to sensual temptation. The book of 1 Thessalonians tells us to abstain from every form of evil. If the act of embracing influences us to sin, then we certainly want to refrain from it. There have been many illegal affairs in the workplace that started from a simple embrace. The attraction started long before the embracing; however, the evil one who also watches what we do, saw when the first seed was planted. Sometimes the flesh is weak and is often not strong enough to refrain from embracing and other forms of temptations.

> Abstain from all appearance of evil. (1 Thessalonians 5:22)

Here are some other scriptures to help us to refrain from embracing so that we can live a righteous life. These are reminders and, coupled with prayer, they can help us to endure this season.

> For we have not a high priest which cannot be touched with the feeling of our infirmities; but was in all points tempted like as we are, yet without sin. (Hebrews 4:15)

> And lead us not into temptation, but deliver us from evil: For thine is the kingdom, and the power, and the glory, for ever. Amen. (Matthew 6:13)

> Watch and pray, that ye enter not into temptation: the spirit indeed is willing, but the flesh is weak. (Matthew 26:41)

> Let not sin therefore reign in your mortal body, that ye should obey it in the lusts thereof. Neither yield ye your members as instruments of unrighteousness unto sin: but yield yourselves unto God, as those that are alive from the dead, and your members as instruments of righteousness unto God. For sin shall not have dominion over you: for ye are not under the law, but under grace. (Romans 6:12–14)

6: A time to get, and a time to lose; a time to keep, and a time to cast away

A Time to Get

This scripture in the King James Version of the Bible reads, "a time to get," but the NIV and other versions read, "a time to search, or seek." I particularly like Merriam's action definition: "to gain possession of; to seek out and obtain."[36] This is so befitting for what our actions should be when seeking God. As believers, we should not only seek God, but find Him. Prayer is only one channel to get in God's presence. An intercessor's aim is to seek God's presence, and therefore His face when lifting our voice in prayer.

> When thou saidst, Seek ye my face; my heart said unto thee, Thy face, Lord, will I seek. (Psalm 27:8)

> And ye shall seek me, and find me, when ye shall search for me with all your heart. (Jeremiah 29:13)

A time to get is a season to not only seek God, but rest in His presence. When this happens, we receive revelation, wisdom, and knowledge. I believe that God moves us into this season at the appointed time when worry, frustration, distress and other emotional states become too much in our lives. At times, the workplace can be a very stressful and demanding environment, and if we do not find a way of escape, it can only worsen over time. When this happens, there is an examination process that needs to take place. If we do not take time to examine the root-cause of our situation, it can overwhelm us.

This season allows for this examination process to take place because the focus changes from yourself to God. Once we spend time in Him, we are able to see more clearly, and we are able to hear and respond with better clarity. The Bible tells us that if we seek the kingdom of God first, all things will be added to us. This has been proven in many cases. When I seek God first, my answers and instructions are made known to me. Now, it is up to me whether or not I take heed of them (free will), but they are given.

> But seek ye first the kingdom of God, and his righteousness; and all these things shall be added unto you. (Matthew 6:33)

I have experienced this season on several occasions. One time comes to mind when I had to realize that I needed some closer time with God. I worked in a demanding environment that sometimes caused stress. This was the job I begged God for: I wanted to work at this place no matter what the cost because I had a specific view about this company. The first time I applied for the job, I was not selected and was very disappointed about it. I felt as though I had failed myself by not being hired. But some time later, I received a call with a job offer, and I was happy. At first, everything was new, and I was enjoying my new position, but over time things begin to change, and I became less excited about working there. At that time, I felt that my relationship with God was good and I prayed very often about the workplace. However, as things began to change considerably, I found myself in a distressed state most of the time. I did not want to walk away from the job, especially after pleading with God for it. My thoughts were that God needed to move the people who were making my experience hard; clearly, that was not the case.

There was more I needed from God, but I was not taking the intimate time needed so that I could hear from Him. Instead, I was getting advice from other sources, meaning I was talking to others about my situation, rather than to God. Later, I came to realize that although He gave me the job, it was only for a season. Many times, we have our own plans, but they do not match up to God's plan, which is a good thing because we would really mess some things up!

My assignment in that workplace was complete, but I was still trying to hold on to it. My assumption was that I needed to remain there in order to get to my next milestone in life. We assume a lot of things without consulting God. Long story short, that season ended and my next season began: a time to get.

This season is an opportunity to really key into what God has been trying to show you throughout your process of distress. After spending some time seeking God in meditation, He helped me remember every step of the process I had been through so that He could reveal some things to me. I was trying to pick and choose my seasons based on my own intellect.

The discomforts I endured were intentional—God allowed certain things to happen to help me in the process of letting go. When all is well it makes it harder to let go—this is called our comfort zone. We all want to be the planners of our life, but contrary to our belief, our life was already mapped out before we were born. God is constantly reminding us of this when our plans do not work as expected.

In our workplaces, we encounter many different people and scenarios in the course of a day. At times we are faced with diverse circumstances that can cause us to respond in a negative manner. The workplace is not excluded from trials and tribulation; the difference is how we respond. Through prayer and meditation, we can find an inner peace that helps us when we are faced with adversity. A time to get is an opportunity to draw near to God so we can see Him in a deeper light.

Let's look at the Hebrew translation for the word get, which is baqash (baw-kash). It means "to search out in any form, including worship and prayer; to strive after; sought for and desire." [37] A season to get is a great invitation to draw near to our heavenly Father and build a closer relationship with Him. There's always room to get closer. From a spiritual perspective, this season is to help us grow as we seek and find a deeper relationship with God in our lives.

> Then there was a famine in the days of David three years, year after year; and David enquired of the Lord. And the Lord answered, (1 Samuel 21:1)

> And I say unto you, Ask, and it shall be given you; seek, and ye shall find; knock, and it shall be opened unto you. For every one that asketh receiveth; and he that seeketh

findeth; and to him that knocketh it shall be opened. (Luke 11:9–10)

For everyone who asks receives; the one who seeks finds; and to the one who knocks, the door will be opened. (Matthew 7:8 NIV)

Luke and Matthew both add a little more to the context as they bring together three parallelisms to approach God:

1. Ask—given;
2. Seek—find;
3. Knock—opened.

All of these options are available to those who desire to "get" in the presence of God. The presence of God is not driven by a specific locality or environment; it can also be considered as a state of mind. Prayer and worship can be exercised from anywhere, not just in a church or structured place of worship. When Jesus was in the Garden of Gethsemane he entered into a prayer state of mind as he sought the Father. We can seek the presence of God even in the workplace. Your state of mind is controlled by you. Situations and circumstances can attempt to dominate your mind-set, but they will only succeed after you have given them your consent.

We spend so much time in the workplace, and without prayer and supplication we will find that when adversity arises we are not equipped to handle the pressure. This has happened on many occasions when there is a separation from assignments on jobs. Some people are not prepared when someone pulls the plug on a job. No matter what the reason is, depending on the mind-set of the individual, they may not be able to be at peace with the decision and therefore will react negatively.

I can remember when I experienced a separation from a work assignment and I was not surprised by the decision— many things do not come as a shocking surprise when you have a personal relationship with our Father in heaven. When you are in a relationship with God—meaning talking, praying and worshipping with Him on a regular basis —He always warns you about what is to come. We may not want to accept, but we have no choice really. However, it is good to be prepared.

In this situation, there were others who were doing some things that had a direct impact on the company's work standards, yet I was the one who was being separated from the company. Although I was ready when the notice was given to me, I still had to connect with God because I wanted peace with this new season. I began to talk to the Lord about what had happened and how I felt that the decision was unfair; I asked God why it seemed as though the impious were being favored. Well, God did not answer right away. I had to endure the rollercoaster of thoughts, replaying the movie over and over in my mind, until one day it was revealed. The season to seek/get with God was getting ready to change.

The Holy Spirit had a soft conversation with me. Before I tell you what He said, I want you to know that I was not in a prayer position; I was not in a church, but merely standing in my bedroom when He began to speak.

He said, "Many people cannot handle separation from their jobs, and this has resulted in tragedy. You have been here before, and once again I gave you this season for such a time as this. Not for you, but for my glory. Write, that it may help others when they are faced with changes of seasons."

God had not only equipped me but had chosen me to write this book. The hands in which this assignment lands are already ordained by Him. I am grateful for all of my seasons, and my delight is to share them with you.

A Time to Lose

The second season mentioned in Ecclesiastes 3:6 is a time to lose. The word lose in this verse is identified as "to wander or go astray."[38] The Hebrew word for lose is abad (aw-bad), which means "to wander away from"; [39] in other words, lose oneself, or break. Other Bible translations read, "a time to give up."

There is another scripture that says whosoever will save their life will lose it. This term in Greek is directed as a message from Jesus to those who hold onto earthly things as their security for salvation, only to find that at the closing of life's curtain, they lose. However, in contrast, the second part of the verse speaks about those who lose their life for the sake of Christ will be saved; meaning to give up (lose) the earthly things in order to gain eternal life. There is absolutely nothing on this earth that is greater than having eternal life.

Often times when we think of losing something as a negative, we must weigh the cost. When we lose something that prevents us from gaining something far more valuable, such as everlasting life, there is no comparison. Sometimes, to lose is to gain.

> For whosoever will save his life shall lose it: but whosoever will lose his life for my sake, the same shall save it. (Luke 9:24–25)

In this season, to lose is to remove things that are preventing us from fulfilling our purpose. Satan's goal is to tempt us with worldly, fleshly things that can cause us to forfeit the greater reward. Remember, that's what he did to Jesus, therefore he will tempt us also. Most of his tactics are the works of the flesh. Galatians 5:19–21 outlines them in the Bible and says that they are clearly evident: simply put, visible, manifest, conspicuous or clear as day, and we all should recognize them.

> Now the works of the flesh are manifest, which are these; Adultery, fornication, uncleanness, lasciviousness, Idolatry, witchcraft, hatred, variance, emulations, wrath, strife, seditions, heresies, envyings,

murders, drunkenness, revellings, and such like: of the which I tell you before, as I have also told you in time past, that they which do such things shall not inherit the kingdom of God. (Galatians 5:19–21)

The things listed above, or as the scripture says, "And such like," these are spiritual manifestations driven from the works of our flesh. I call them spiritual, fiery spears directed to destroy our purpose. Now, these are things that require a greater spiritual surgery to remove. Usually, there are certain things that attach us to these works of the flesh, but there comes a time to lose those things and God uses that season for this process. Some of them could be a workplace or places we go, people we need to get away from, or things we attach ourselves to.

These manifestations exist in abundance in most workplaces. When these works are in operation, they can infect the environment we work in. One work of the flesh promotes more works of the flesh. Remember, Satan works in multiplication also. He knows our desires; then he presents the bate to us. Some people are stronger than others and can resist the enemy, but there are some that are feeble and give in. The good thing about it is God gives us an opportunity (season) to lose those things that derail us from our purpose.

I notice that adultery is at the top of the list. All are sinful, but this one is included as one of the Ten Commandments that God plainly spelled out. This must have been in full operation even back then, so this must be one of Satan's top picks to tempt people with. This manifestation of the flesh has many branches that stem from it: deception, lust, dishonesty, to name just a few. In some workplaces, there are greater opportunities to fall into this trap than others, but once you lose the appetite and stop feeding off that root, the branches of that spirit dry up.

I believe we all have personal experiences that relate to the Matthew 5:28 scripture, which says, "That anyone who looks at someone lustfully has already committed adultery." Most of us have viewed this from a sexual perspective, but it is much deeper. Like most works of the flesh, it has a spiritual root that aims to disconnect your spiritual cord with God.

Just when you think, you have conquered something's, the enemy throws a curb ball. Being transparent is a great part of my writing and spiritual growth for God to use my testimonies to help others. Years ago in the workplace, there was a man, and we were both were Christians but he was married. It came a time when we started having a lot of conversations with one another which we thought was innocent. We shared things with one another and the work relationship grew stronger, but we did not realize was the non-work relationship was growing as well. We did not want to admit at first that we were becoming attracted to each other. But it was not long before Satan really turned up the fire in my thoughts and, the more we both tried to act like the attraction did not exist, the worse it got. These rapid thoughts were building an invisible relationship that was growing stronger than any tangible one. I had never experienced something as strong as this before. I've had physical relationships before, but this was different: it consumed my thoughts, and my imagination was out of control. One day he and I talked about it because both of us were experiencing the same thing. We could not explain it and we wondered how this could be, since we had never touched or physically interacted with one other. There was a power drawing us to each other. It became a spiritual battle. Mind you, it did not start out like this, but grew over time to the point that it felt like we had fallen deeply in love. We never had a sexual conversation, physical encounter nor kissed one another. What we did do was talk to each other whenever we had an opportunity. It was crazy and we could not explain it—but it existed. Day and night, it weighed down on me. I prayed for it to go away, but it did not. I would do whatever I could to avoid the person so that these feelings would go away, but they only grew stronger. I could not talk about it with others because I was ashamed and it was ungodly, and if the secret (deception-key) got out, it could really do a lot of damage. This was Satan's goal.

God had to intervene. He answered my prayer and changed my season. It became a time to lose. I had to lose something in order to help me to overcome that spiritual adversity. Adultery in this context can be viewed symbolically, of those who are drawn away by a Jezebel-type solicitation or proposition spirit. This was why the spirit was so strong and influential. The adultery spirit is a counterfeiter with a mission to draw us further from God. The fiery spear that Satan used was a destructive tactic, but God won! To prepare me for the spiritual surgery to deal with that spirit, I had to lose (give up) that workplace. In the season to lose, it cost me something, but in losing, there was a great gain. He removed me from that workplace, and the thoughts and feelings all died. If I had stayed, it would have forfeited my blessing in my next season of purpose.

This also brings to mind the narrative about Samson's encounter with Delilah. Although they had a physical relationship, the spiritual aspect was raging out of control because of his purpose and assignment on the earth. It was the same spirit operating within Sampson—strong, powerful, but deadly. Our prayer should be to welcome the season to lose because it could save your life.

It may not be our intent to participate in any of these works, nevertheless they can show up in your life unexpectedly. Please understand that no one is exempt from the traps Satan sets for us. There comes a time when it is necessary to lose things that are causing us not to grow and prosper in areas of our lives. We must remember how important our purpose is. It may not be of this magnitude, but I was led to write about it to expose the enemy.

A Time to Keep

The term to keep in this passage has a Hebrew meaning, shamar (shaw-mar). It means "to hedge about, guard, to protect, attend to or watch over even as a watchman—from the point of view of tending to, or taking care of."[40] The first occurrence in the Bible was in Genesis 2:15 of how God put Adam in the garden to keep watch over and guard it. Adam's mandate to keep the garden should not be taken lightly, as this was a great and powerful assignment. We can glean so many life lessons from his season in the garden of Eden.

When we view Adam's job or work functions, we see him as a gardener, a plantsman, who had to be very skilled and proficient, yet circumspectly, and sure in his assignment. I believe that he was probably the greatest horticulturist; he was in charge of keeping some of God's first creations. When God gives us something to watch over, He not only equips us to do the job but makes us accountable in the position also.

Reflecting on one of the definitions of keep is putting a hedge about it. This term can be referenced as a means of protection or defense to prevent movement or action. [41]As a gardener, one can put a fence or set a hedge around a garden in order to protect from it from something that can cause damage or unwanted entry. The gardener is the watchman over His garden.

Your workplace can be viewed symbolically as your garden: a place where there is planting, grooming, and reaping toward a great harvest. Your garden is a carved-out piece of God's master landscape, created by His divine purpose. We are watchmen over our gardens. We are to carefully keep watch over the garden to prevent unwanted guests, pestilence, serpents, and other demonic instruments that could prevent purpose and fulfillment in the workplace.

The hedge about keeps a dense view, and if anything is out of place, it will stick out like a thorn or weeds. As we know, weeds and briars can show up in the most beautiful gardens and will grow in patches, a stem or a massive form. They can be thorny or prickly, waiting to cause pain when someone touches them. No workplace or garden is exempt from these annoying, undesirable obstacles.

Gardening is not an easy task or assignment. The more we cut our personal lawn and trim our shrubbery, the more it keeps growing with the demand for more care. We put down weed killer, but weeds come right back; there is always some new growth of non-plant-family member insisting on coexisting with the others. We remove one and another comes back—it is constant work to keep and maintain. The same with our workplace. There can be daily changes that require more trimming to keep us on course with our purpose.

Like Adam, we are to watch over and tend to the place God has assigned us to. We can learn a valuable lesson from what happened to Adam in the garden when the evilness in the serpent showed up in the garden. We are to watch and pray at all times so that when Satan shows up in our garden/workplace, an alarm sounds within us to recognize that spirit quickly and deal with it accordingly. Satan's goal is to destroy by enticing us with temptation. Here is a list of cautions to help you discern his cunning game plan:

1. Satan's tactics—his approach comes under a lie (Gen 3:1; John 12:6)
2. Satan's voice—opposite of God's instruction, statutes, commands, and will (Gen 3; Matt 16:23)
3. Satan's schemes—deception is key as an imposter, fraudster, play-actor (Eph 6:10–18; 1 John 4:1–3)
4. Satan's strategy—he watches for his entry point (Mark 5:13; Mark 9:25; John 12:40)
5. Satan's plan—accuser of the brethren (us) day and night (Rev 12:10)
6. Satan's aim—to destroy, and our end be destruction (1 Thess 1:8–9; John 10:10)

Watch ye and pray, lest ye enter into temptation. The spirit truly is ready, but the flesh is weak. (Mark 14:38)

I believe that God has imparted some of the gardening characteristics in us. He wants us to be in tune with the timing of His nature, receiving the knowledge of sowing and reaping as the times and seasons present themselves to us. Gardeners must be patient in between seasons. Some seasons are longer than others, and they are never the same. The process in each is always different to what we expect. The time table is solely dependent upon God's plan unless you enforce your free will.

To keep can also be viewed as a natural instinct given to mankind. As a mother, I felt the internal intuition to watch over my children when they were born. I had a strong sense to keep them safe and protect them as they grew. Even now they are young adults, I still share in on the protection plan, just not at the same level. Likewise, God is our keeper. He protects us from danger seen and unseen. David describes God as a sun and shield. When God can trust you "to keep" what He has given you, it is a blessing. I believe when God can trust us with what He gives us, He will enlarge our territory even more. I like what Zephaniah says: "He will rejoice over thee with singing." A question for you to meditate on: what has God given you to keep or be a watchman over for a season?

As we go through the season to keep, as a type of gardener, we should also have a mind-set of growth expectation from our garden. What we sow, we reap—remembering that the reaping is always greater than the seed sown. When we plant good seeds in our garden, it should be with great anticipation to yield a harvest. The thief is always lurking to steal your harvest. Continued prayer over your workplace is an excellent cadence to help nurture, water and most of all keep your hedges round about to help keep the enemy out.

A Time to Cast Away

A time to cast away is a season to throw out, down or away. The Hebrew word is shalak (shaw-lak), which means "to throw, fling, cast or overthrow." Shalak can also be considered as rejection.[42] When you think of throwing something away, it conveys a sense of abandonment; of discarding something, which can point to rejection.

This season can have two unique processes: one to cast out something or someone that is physical, and two, to cast out something that is spiritual. The first one can be a very impactful process depending on the circumstances that drive the casting away. When you experience a casting away in the workplace, it can be an emotional as well as a spiritual process.

There is a biblical reference that demonstrates the sensitivity of being cast away. Hagar was the mother of Abraham's son Ishmael. She was a bond servant to Sarah (Abraham's wife). They all lived in the same camp/workplace. After Isaac was born, and once he came of age, Sarah told Abraham to cast away Hagar and her son Ishmael so there would be no interruption with the inheritance for their son Isaac.

> And Sarah saw the son of Hagar the Egyptian, which she had born unto Abraham, mocking. Wherefore she said unto Abraham, Cast out this bondwoman and her son: for the son of this bondwoman shall not be heir with my son, even with Isaac. And the thing was very grievous in Abraham's sight because of his son. (Genesis 21:9–11)

Some separations can be very hard even when they come about by a mutual agreement. However, when the separation such as being cast out comes as a surprise or without choice, there can be a tremendous hurt that takes place. This type of season opens the door for the rejection seed to be planted. This has happened many times in the workplace, where people have experienced rejection due to loss of a job. Feeling cast out of the workplace for personal, unfair or financial reasons, some have experienced great hardship and have struggled to find forgiveness toward those who made the casting out decision. The process during this season is the not only an opportunity to see the will of God in operation, but also to apply the healing in order to recover.

Abraham was aggrieved by Sarah's demand; he was concerned because Ishmael was his son also. But God spoke to Abraham to comfort him because there was a promise for both of his sons: Isaac would get the inheritance, but Ishmael would also be blessed.

Even though God spoke to Abraham concerning the promise, the decision to cast out Hagar and her son was not overturned. She and Ishmael departed from their home and place of work into the wilderness, where they wandered. Hagar was terrified they would not survive. Feeling hopeless and not knowing what else to do, she ended up casting her son under some shrubs and leaving him there because she did not want to see her son die.

> And Abraham rose up early in the morning, and took bread, and a bottle of water, and gave it unto Hagar, putting it on her shoulder, and the child, and sent her away: and she departed, and wandered in the wilderness of Beersheba. And the water was spent in the bottle, and she cast the child under one of the shrubs. (Genesis 21:14–15)

I can only imagine how Hagar's mind was full of bitterness toward those who had cast her out. This was an unexpected change in her life. One day everything is going okay in the workplace and at home, then someone hosts a meeting about you that will change your entire livelihood. In most cases, we are not included in those meetings...The story does not indicate the timeline from the delivery of the message to when Hagar actually had to leave the camp, but it was the next segment of action according to the scriptures.

The pressure of being cast away, or removed from your workplace can send you into a wilderness state. The wilderness usually represents testing ground, which is a process in itself. This state has a way of playing on the mind, and at times there can be a daily process just to keep a sound mind. When life-changing events happen to us, it is a must that we remain at peace in our minds. The enemy will work on your mind to the tenth power if you allow him. Satan uses tactics like replaying the event back and forth in your head until it consumes all your thoughts. The best method to use against this tactic is to pray positive prayers that are full of promise and to worship God no matter what. Be like Job—pray! We cannot allow the enemy to keep us stuck and wallow in the pain and change of life.

When you are in a wilderness process, you cannot always see your way out. This is because we get stuck in the past, preventing us from being able to view the new future that God has for us. While in most wilderness states, our future is masked by the toils and pain of what has happened in the past. Conversely, we should put one foot in front of the other and trust God to take good care of us. His Word is infallible, and it will not return void.

> So shall my word be that goeth forth out of my mouth: it shall not return unto me void, but it shall accomplish that which I please, and it shall prosper in the thing whereto I sent it. (Isaiah 55:11)

In this case, God had already promised Abraham that his son (his seed) would be blessed. Hagar had to connect to the promise that God gave for Ishmael. She was ready to give up when she cast her son under the shrubs. But at the appointed time, God sent His angel to speak with Hagar to encourage her. More so, He opened her eyes to see the well of water. This is why we cannot give up—we must fight for our right to the promises that God has for us.

God is our fountain that never runs dry. When we drink from His well, there is no thirst. Man can do things to dry up a brook, but God is the one who provides the water, and when one dries up, there is another to drink from. There is no lack of God. We cannot give up when we are cast out. Sometimes God allows us to be cast away to push us into our promised future.

> And she went, and sat her down over against him a good way off, as it were a bow shot: for she said, Let me not see the death of the child. And she sat over against him, and lift up her voice, and wept. And God heard the voice of the lad; and the angel of God called to Hagar out of heaven, and said unto her, What aileth thee, Hagar? fear not; for God hath heard the voice of the lad where he is. Arise, lift up the lad, and hold him in thine hand; for I will make him a great nation. And God opened her eyes, and she saw a well of water; and she went, and filled the bottle with water, and gave the lad drink. And God was with the lad; and he grew, and dwelt in the wilderness, and became an archer. (Genesis 21:16–20)

To cast away something that is spiritual also has a unique process; it is called letting go. We carry more than we should. We can always rely on David to lend inspired and meaningful words of encouragement.

In Psalms 55:22, it says, "Cast thy burden upon the Lord." This means we can give all of our burdens to the Lord God. We can lay them down, throw or fling them; just so long as we give them over to Him, the work can be done. God wants us worry-free. In the workplace, there are many things that manifest during the course of the day—some good and some bad, but the good thing is we do not have to carry them with us. The weight of carrying burdens that do not belong to us makes our journey heavier than it has to be.

Give your burdens to God and let Him be God and work through the madness. He is so much better at working it out if we allow His will to be done. Some burdens we pick up because we feel a need to fix or undo something or someone in our own power. When we do this, "letting go" becomes the issue as opposed to casting the burden over to God. One of the most important things we will learn in life is that we cannot change people. Some people simply need a spiritual heart transplant, and only God can do that. If God holds the heart of a king in His hand, then surely, He can manage to turn the heart of those in the home, school, church or workplace.

You can lighten the weight of your situation today by casting burdens upon the Lord and leaving them there. We can continue to pray even while God is in the middle of it. Situations and circumstances in the workplace can seem important, but our position is to pray for God to lighten the load—because His yoke is easy.

> Cast thy burden upon the Lord, and he shall sustain thee: he shall never suffer the righteous to be moved. (Psalms 55:22)

> For my yoke is easy, and my burden is light. (Matthew 11:30)

7: A time to rend, and a time to sew; a time to keep silence, and a time to speak

A Time to Rend

To rend means "to carry out an act of tearing or splitting; or when something becomes split or torn." [43]The Hebrew word for rend is qara (kaw-rah), which means "rend or rent, lit. tear away, cut out"—like tearing one's clothing. This type of act was commonly used to show an expression of grief. [44]

To rend your clothing was a physical way of voicing one's sorrows or heartache, and sometimes even anger. This is a tangible reaction and expresses a desire to release. To rend something that has been sewed together takes some force because of the intent of pulling it apart. Once the garment is torn, it no longer holds its form. You may attempt to patch it, but it is rarely the same again.

We can also view the rending as a prophetic act. The veil being rent when Jesus was on the cross was a sign of opening the new way to our God, our Father in heaven. The curtain was torn from top to bottom. This was not an expression of grief, but of great awakening.

At times, the word rend is used symbolically to emphasize separation, like in 1 Kings 11:30 when the prophet Ahijah tore Jeroboam's new garment into twelve portions, representing the forthcoming division of the tribes of Israel. The act of rending was a spiritual separation and a change in season for Solomon.

There will be appointed times when God will use separation to bless others. In this case, Jeroboam was given kingdoms that were taken away (rent) from Solomon. Our God is sovereign and will do what He pleases, especially for those who keep His commands and statues. Why do you think history repeats itself? Is it because we keep making the same mistakes over and over again rather than learning from the past? God has to keep showing us who He is and how His words never change nor fall to the ground. The day and time may change, but seasons remain the same. We are to learn from our forefathers. The testimonies in the Bible give a greater understanding of God's goodness. This is why the Bible was written—so we could have access to learning about life as we live.

Regarding this situation of Solomon, it was repeated history that he could have learned from. Saul was the King of Israel before his father, King David, and had the same thing happen to him. God rent the kingdom from him and gave it to David for not keeping His statutes.

> And Samuel said unto him, The Lord hath rent the kingdom of Israel from thee this day, and hath given it to a neighbour of thine, that is better than thou. (1 Samuel 15:28)

Personally, I really do not understand how someone can choose not to believe that the testimonies in the Bible are the inspired words of God. This is why it is so important to build a relationship with our Father in heaven; so that when we hear truth, our spirit within bears witness to it. He shows Himself true throughout history. I love the fact that He does not change.

The season to rend can be viewed in 1 Kings chapter 11. The passage or segment gives the roadmap of how we can hold a position and then have it taken from us. This example shows how God was angry with Solomon because his heart was turned from Him by not keeping His commands. Now, he had seven hundred wives, princesses, and three hundred concubines. One can probably come to the conclusion that Solomon could have some lustful issues with women. These types of desires take ownership of the heart. He even allowed some of the women to lure him to worship other gods.

In verse 13, the threat was made known, that God would rend away (tear) the kingdom from him. I believe that God warns us before He takes action, especially if things we do are not pleasing in His sight.

> Howbeit I will not rend away all the kingdom; but will give one tribe to thy son for David my servant's sake, and for Jerusalem's sake which I have chosen. (1 Kings 11:13)

In the workplace, we can experience both the bitter and sweet seasons. Some can be somewhat of a bitter taste when a shift happens. Have you ever worked in a place where an organizational change takes place unexpectedly? In the corporate world, they are called reorgs, and they can happen at any time. At times, they can make people very bitter, especially when positions change quickly. One day a person can be ruling their worldly kingdoms, and the next moment it has been rent from them.

Let's view some of the scriptures in 1 Kings 11:28–39 to help us understand more about the rend season from a prophetic perspective.

God reveals who you are to others

And the man Jeroboam was a mighty man of valour: and Solomon seeing the young man that he was industrious, he made him ruler over all the charge of the house of Joseph. (1 Kings 11:28)

Shifting of season begins in the prophetic realm (foretold)

And it came to pass at that time when Jeroboam went out of Jerusalem, that the prophet Ahijah the Shilonite found him in the way; and he had clad himself with a new garment; and they two were alone in the field: And Ahijah caught the new garment that was on him, and rent it in twelve pieces:

And he said to Jeroboam, Take thee ten pieces: for thus saith the Lord, the God of Israel, Behold, I will rend the kingdom out of the hand of Solomon, and will give ten tribes to thee: (But he shall have one tribe for my servant David's sake, and for Jerusalem's sake, the city which I have chosen out of all the tribes of Israel:) (1 Kings 11:29–32)

At the appointed time Jeroboam was in the field wearing a new garment that the prophet used prophetically to demonstrate the rending of the kingdom from the hands of King Solomon.

What provoked the rend season

Because that they have forsaken me, and have worshipped Ashtoreth the goddess of the Zidonians, Chemosh the god of the Moabites, and Milcom the god of the children of Ammon, and have not walked in my ways, to do that which is right in mine eyes, and to keep my statutes and my judgments, as did David his father.

Howbeit I will not take the whole kingdom out of his hand: but I will make him prince all the days of his life for David my servant's sake, whom I chose, because he kept my commandments and my statutes: But I will take the kingdom out of his son's hand, and will give it unto thee, even ten tribes. (1 Kings 11:33–35)

Solomon swayed away from doing what was right in God's eyes, and as a result, his season changed as well Jeroboam's season. Sometimes our season can impact more than one person.

God still shows mercy in our seasons

And unto his son will I give one tribe, that David my servant may have a light always before me in Jerusalem, the city which I have chosen me to put my name there.

> And I will take thee, and thou shalt reign according to all that thy soul desireth, and shalt be king over Israel.
>
> And it shall be, if thou wilt hearken unto all that I command thee, and wilt walk in my ways, and do that is right in my sight, to keep my statutes and my commandments, as David my servant did; that I will be with thee, and build thee a sure house, as I built for David, and will give Israel unto thee. And I will for this afflict the seed of David, but not for ever. (1 Kings 11:36–39)

Although God took the kingdom from Solomon, it was only for a season, on the condition that Solomon kept God's commands, statutes, and did what was right. The promise that God made to the house of David was still in effect. Whatever God promises you, He will do, but it is up to us to maintain what God requires. Seasons do not last forever, but what happens in the seasons surely impacts the outcome.

God can take (rend) from one person and use it to bless another. In the example above, this was a transfer of wealth for a season. It is a great reminder that God is the one who gives the increase—and the decrease as well. He is always watching to see how we treat one another and if we are doing what is pleasing in His sight. You cannot get around it.

One day, people will understand that God's eyes are like a rolling-camera on us as long as we are here on the earth. Nothing we do is secret, because God is all-knowing and all-seeing. The Bible tells us in Revelation that we will all be judged for our deeds. We are accountable for what we do and how we treat others.

The rending season can happen at any time. God has not given us positions in any workplace for personal gain. Although you may reap a harvest during a season, it can change without notice. Remember, Solomon was the richest man ever, but God took his kingdoms from him. We are not exempt from the season of rending.

A Time to Sew

This season represents a time to sew together. The word sew signifies "to unite or fasten by stitches; to close or enclose by sewing." A person can practice or engage in the act of sewing. To sew requires an action. Merriam-Webster simply explains sewing as making or repairing something.[45] Strong's does not give much information on this, but the Hebrew word is taphar (taw-far), "a primitive root, to sew, meaning women that sew together." Some other related words to sew are mend, repair, knit, or stitch. [46]

This word is first mentioned in the Bible in Genesis 3:7, when Adam and Eve sewed together leaves to hide their nakedness.

> And the eyes of them both were opened, and they knew that they were naked; and they sewed fig leaves together, and made themselves aprons. (Genesis 3:7)

In this case, Adam and Eve wanted to cover up their physical bodies after realizing for the first time that they were naked. The truth is they were naked all along, but it had not been revealed to them until they disobeyed God. In reading this, I asked this question: "If they sewed together fig leaves to cover up, then why did they still hide from God?" The KJV scripture above says they made themselves aprons. Well, aprons provide only a partial covering. So, they were trying to cover only a part of their bodies. Therefore, when their eyes were opened, they could see their gender, which is probably why they tried to cover up. How many times have we tried to sew something together to hide from the view of others?

I believe that when we try to cover up something, we often forget that we could never hide from God. He is all-knowing and all-seeing. I would also assume we look just like Adam and Eve did when we try to cover something that we think is hidden from God.

A time to sew can be a season of knitting and weaving things together to provide a covering. Although this season is positioned in the scripture after the rend season, it does not necessarily mean it follows that season but can rather come before. At times, sewing things together can be temporary. Some stitches hold together well, and others come apart easily. This can depend on the quality or strength of the stich or the skill of the sewer (seamstress/tailor). The one that comes apart is like the world's thread, but when God is our tailor doing the stitching, it is being sewn into our purpose.

This season can be viewed also as a time of sewing the Word into our lives. Allowing the inspired word to be sewn into our hearts and minds. The scriptures can be refreshing to our spirits. Receiving revelation is like sewing a new cloth on an old garment. At times our stitching needs to be repaired in order to renew our strength in God. Revelation brings that strength.

> No man also seweth a piece of new cloth on an old garment: else the new piece that filled it up taketh away from the old, and the rent is made worse. (Mark 2:21)

From a spiritual view, we can see Jesus as the new cloth on the old garment or covenant. The new offers us a personal relationship with our Father in heaven as opposed to living under the Old Testament law. The new cloth is like the "Good News" because we have the forgiveness of sin through Christ Jesus. The law condemned us but Christ came so we could have life and have it more abundantly.

In the next verse, Mark presents a strong metaphor of a wineskin to talk about applying the new to the old. Wineskins were bags used to put wine in and were normally made of animal skin, mainly goat, with strong stitches around them to hold the contents. Wine will usually expand as it is fermented, and when poured into an old wineskin, the wineskin can burst at the seams because it is not strong enough to hold new wine. Again, putting the new into the old can cause things to come apart.

The wine represents God's covenant of grace. When we renew our mind to receive this covenant, we are able to hold and apply the new wine to our lives. However, if we choose to pour the new into the old wineskins (like the law) we can find ourselves busted at the seams—leaving us in need of repair. When we reject what God has put in place for us, it makes our way hard because His grace is sufficient for us to have an abundant life.

> And no one puts new wine into old wineskins; or else the new wine bursts the wineskins, the wine is spilled,

and the wineskins are ruined. But new wine must be put into new wineskins. (Mark 2:22 NKJV)

God uses the workplace in many forms. In the season to sew we should recognize that God is always sewing things together for our good. Renewing your mind is a key principle because it can change your view of how you perceive something. I grew up in church, and as far back as I can remember, tithes and offerings of money were a controversial topic. I believe that most people have either questioned or misunderstood the principle behind giving unto God. The scriptures clearly tell us to give, and if we are going to believe what they say, then we must accept all of it. For me, I did not have a problem with giving, but I lacked the understanding to trust God in my giving and to apply it to every area of my life.

God tested my giving with a challenge. Now, there is a scripture that I found a challenge but which changed my perspective about giving:

> Bring ye all the tithes into the storehouse, that there may be meat in mine house, and prove me now herewith, saith the Lord of hosts, if I will not open you the windows of heaven, and pour you out a blessing, that there shall not be room enough to receive it. (Malachi 3:10)

One day, about twelve years ago, I was driving in my car, having a conversation with God, and I told Him that I wanted to make over $100k a year. My mind-set at that time was that I did not have the type of degree to support making those figures, and people in my workplaces constantly reminded me of that.

Once people try to place you in a position of their choosing, a sad thing happens: you start to accept that position in your mind instead of accepting what God (our Creator) has purposed for us. A lot of our pre-set thoughts are imparted by others. If we do not take time to revisit how we think, we can find ourselves stuck on old wineskins as opposed to the new abundant living.

After telling God what I wanted, He said to me, "Start tithing like you are already making $100,000 a year." I knew that was God speaking because that thought was far beyond where my mind was.

I said to Him, "Hmm, so how much do I have to give?"—knowing that 10 percent of $100,000 was $10,000. My thoughts went directly to the $10,000 and I found myself in panic mode, thinking I can't give that much! I was feeling the anxiety of being stretched because I had not given on that scale before. Yet, I wanted God to put me on that scale. My wineskin (mind-set) was old and too small. If I wanted to receive the new increase, I needed a new wineskin sewed together (renewed mind-set) so I could start thinking on the increased level before I actually received it.

The first course of action is always faith. The scripture says, prove me now. So, I started using my mind to perform the calculation I needed to put the plan into action. I had to change my salary in spirit, as though that was how much I was actually getting paid. The Holy Spirit said start from the end then come back to the beginning. I divided $100,000 into the number of my pay cycles in that year to get the total amount to give from each paycheck. Even though it was hard, and at times and I came up short with other bills, I kept giving until it became natural, and was no longer a struggle. I was determined to stay on course with the challenge to fulfill the scripture that says, "prove me now."

Then after some time had passed, I did not think about the challenge. I was not watching the return. God began to open doors of opportunity in the workplace; He closed some doors and opened others. Each new door was an entry of increase. I must tell you that I was not focused on the challenge as God was moving. It was not until one day I was looking at my taxes and the Holy Spirit brought back to my remembrance my conversation with God in the car that day. As I looked through my documents, I realized that I made over $100,000 in that year.

All I could say was, "Wow, God! You proved yourself true in your Word."

I was overjoyed in my spirit with great love.

God took time to sew together some very valuable principles in that season. The more money He gave me, the more my mind changed about money. It was like my view changed from "my money," to "God's money." I realized that the money really does not belong to me, but to Him. Therefore, it made it easier to handle and I did not miss it once it was released. My mind-set changed from letting it rule me with all of my desires, to ruling it for God's desires. This way of thinking is definitely about a new wineskin being tightly stitched together to hold the challenges of faith and trusting God.

God said it, I believed, and God did it. However, the challenge does not stop there, but continues. The more God gives, the larger the giving becomes. The challenge is to remain faithful in your giving as the amount increases. I am waiting to have the opportunity to give $100,000 or $100 million. There are no limits to what God can do. I encourage you to put your faith into action and accept the challenge, and allow God to prove His Word in your life.

> This season of sewing was a process of great change for me. When I look back, all I can say is that I never missed a beat. Nothing was cut off or taken away, and the fruit was great. Malachi 3:11 is the second part of my testimony:

> And I will rebuke the devourer for your sakes, and he shall not destroy the fruits of your ground; neither shall your vine cast her fruit before the time in the field, saith the Lord of hosts. (Malachi 3:11)

In our seasonal life, it is good to be reminded how all scripture is given by inspiration of God so we can have what is needed for good works, meaning the Word works for our good.

> All scripture is given by inspiration of God, and is profitable for doctrine, for reproof, for correction, for instruction in righteousness: That the man of God may be perfect, thoroughly furnished unto all good works. (2 Timothy 3:16–17)

The season of sewing is good. When God is sewing our stiches of life together, it is working together for our good for those who love Him. Yielding to God's will, especially in our workplaces, and should reassure us when we are on course with our purpose.

> And we know that all things work together for good to them that love God, to them who are the called according to his purpose. (Romans 8:28)

A Time to Keep Silence

This is one of those seasons that should be frequent in our lives. There is a saying that silence is golden, meaning that at times it is wise to be silent. Chashah (khaw-shaw) is the Hebrew word for silence. It means "to keep quiet or hold peace; be still." [47]One characterization of silence is absence of sound or noise, as in the silence of the night. As a noun, silence could refer to restraining from speech. The verb form is to compel or reduce to silence; to suppress or to cause hostile firing or criticism to cease.

Silence can sometimes be referred to as being still, holding your peace, or being quiet. There are times when we need to withhold our speech. Silence can also be a position of reverence; not speaking enhances our hearing. Not everything requires a response. [48]I heard a young woman teach at a conference once that her parents raised her to believe that if you are not required to speak, then do not: be an observer and listen more.

I call this season of keeping silent, a learning season. Silence enables your listening. Your hearing is clearer and sharper when you are silent. The Spirit of the Lord is always speaking, but it is when we are silent that we can hear Him best. There is strength in listening. Isaiah says our strength is renewed in silence.

> Keep silence before me, O islands; and let the people renew their strength: let them come near; (Isaiah 41:1)

At times there are a multitude of things manifesting in the workplace. Some are good, and some are not so good. The truth (Ecclesiastes 1:9) is there is nothing new under the sun. What we experience has already been experienced before. One thing is for certain: whenever we try to do good, evil is always present.

What I have found over the years of working is that all jobs are the same. We may hold different positions, and perform different functions, at different geographical locations, but they are all "jobs," with a divine purpose called "work." The same types of spirts exist in them all. What you will encounter on one job, you will encounter on another. It may have a different flavor, but it will operate from the same principle. Sometimes we view things from a lower level, but God works on a higher level. The divine principle should be our starting point, and then we work our way down into the details. If we start with a higher view, then we won't get so caught up in the details, which is all the stuff we encounter in the workplace. The higher view shows us how everything fits together. We are one, and that was and still is God's design. Everything works together for those who love Him (Romans 8:28). Our first approach should always be to understand purpose. When we start here, we learn who God really is as the Creator.

One day I heard my daughter ask, "Why do I keep getting the same type of boss on every job? Why is there the same unfairness, same schisms, but different job titles?"

The fact is people change positions, but the spirit does not unless there is a renewing of the mind. Some will operate under the same spirit no matter where they go: home or work. If they are operating under an evil spirit, that's who they are really working with.

The workplace is not exempt from evil times. There is no time set on when it begins or end. We must endure it until the season changes. When evil presents itself in the workplace, we should be silent with our speech to hear in the spirit. This does not mean stop praying. Prayer and supplication are what helps sustain you. Plus, prayer will open up more revelation for discerning the spirits. We want to hear with clarity. Amos says that the wise are to keep silent during these times.

> Therefore the prudent shall keep silence in that time; for it is an evil time. (Amos 5:13)

Jesus is our role model for when to be silent. During the time when he was captured and taken before Pilate to be crucified, Jesus remained silent. Surely these were evil times he was experiencing. The torture was unbearable, and I believe that there were many types of spirits fully activated in the people accusing him; yet he remained silent. Nevertheless, he was in perfect communication with our Father in heaven. Prayer is a position or posture that is spirit to spirit. No one can ever stop you from praying to the Father.

> And when he was accused of the chief priests and elders, he answered nothing. Then said Pilate unto him, Hearest thou not how many things they witness against thee? And he answered him to never a word; insomuch

> that the governor marvelled greatly. (Matthew 27:12–14)

Our season of silence is toward men not God. We must seek wisdom about when to be silent. Once we discern that evil is present, we enter into a season of silence.

Have you ever regretted saying something in the workplace? Once the words are spoken, they cannot be taken back. Sometimes our spoken words can cause more damage, especially when they are not released at the right time. Discerning before speaking will keep us. There will be times in our workplaces when evil will make its presence known, and how we respond will determine the enemy's next move. When things are turning for the worse, it is probably not good to add fuel to the fire. Words have power—they can penetrate deep beyond the surface. Depending on the nature and content of the words, it can create a footprint in your heart that can remain forever. Rather than create something that is not fruitful and prosperous for us, choose to be silent and be joyful about the things you will learn from being silent. Remember it is a season and it will change.

> But the Lord is in his holy temple: let all the earth keep silence before him. (Habakkuk 2:20)

A Time to Speak

A season where there is a time to speak is to verbalize expressions in the form of words. We use our words to express many thoughts, beliefs, ideas or maybe even judgments. I believe that the importance of speaking is not what we speak but the timing of what it is spoken.

The word speak in Hebrew is dabar (daw-bar).[49] In the verb form, Strong's Concordance mentions that the focus is not only on the matter of spoken message but also on the time and circumstances of what is said. This goes back to the importance of the season or timing of speech. In the Old Testament, the prophets spoke the mind of God with whatever instructions were given. Most of time when God speaks, it comes with instructions and perfect timing. Spoken words can travel through time with divine purposes. They can be words of promise, communion, pronouncement, answer, declaration, proclamation, giving, naming, teaching or even destroying. Speech is one of the most diversified expressions of mankind.

Some may wonder why timing is key to speaking about a matter. At times we can speak prematurely, which can cause havoc or unexpected results; while, on the other hand, our delayed speech can cause us to miss the timing of needed spoken words. Both can have an impact on our destiny.

In general, most people take words for granted. They are viewed as small and powerless, especially when it comes to our destiny. The truth is, our heaven and earth both were and still are governed by words. God spoke His Words into the atmosphere and it impacted all of creation in the beginning. Words are so powerful that they divided the waters and set the sun in the sky, and these things are still in place today. If speaking is not important, then why would the Almighty God speak His words to command the earth and have it respond to what He says?

Genesis 1 tells us that God created man in their image. Man (male and female) are God's design and we were all made from that design. So, if we are made in His image then we have a persona like God to speak words. He also gave man dominion on earth (Genesis 1:26). This why Satan hates us so much, because we are made in His image. He wanted to be like God but could not be.

> And God said, Let us make man in our image, after our likeness: and let them have dominion over the fish of the sea, and over the fowl of the air, and over the cattle, and over all the earth, and over every creeping thing that creepeth upon the earth. So God created man in his own image, in the image of God created he him; male and female created he them. (Genesis 1:26–27)

After God formed Adam, He placed him in his workplace (the garden of Eden) to establish his purpose: to work. Also, God brought every animal to Adam to name (speak) each of them (Genesis 1:19). Again, speaking words into the atmosphere and those names/words are still being dominated today. Communication is a key principle and God expects us to use our words to speak into the atmosphere to govern the things on the earth that He has given us. Things that are good, pure and honest that bring Him glory.

One of the main things that Satan goes after is our words. He wants us to speak irresponsibly, recklessly, or carelessly to keep us off the timing of God's divine will. He knows that we have been created to speak with power, and He also knows that we have the power to change things. This was God's original plan for man. The fall of Adam changed some things, but through Jesus Christ we have our authority on earth to speak things that can cause a manifestation. For one reason, we should except and confess that Jesus Christ is Lord and has been given all authority in heaven and earth (Matthew 28:18). He spoke and said those words to the disciples and those words are still governing today through those who believe.

> And Jesus came and spake unto them, saying, All power is given unto me in heaven and in earth. Go ye therefore, and teach all nations, baptizing them in the name of the Father, and of the Son, and of the Holy Ghost: Teaching them to observe all things whatsoever I have commanded you: and, lo, I am with you always, even unto the end of the world. Amen. (Matthew 28:18–20)

Our words are important, which is why we should be careful what we say. Some words have actions that proceed power, like "go, depart, move." These words have an immediate instruction and action. Notice that whenever Jesus spoke, it was an appointed time to release the words into the atmosphere. His words had authority to take root in the earth.

> For I have not spoken of myself; but the Father which sent me, he gave me a commandment, what I should say, and what I should speak. (John 12:49)

As mentioned in the previous chapter, Jesus was silent when provoked by Satan, but when it was time for him to speak, he spoke with substance. Jesus used his words to remind Satan of God's written word because it was, and still is the living word. I add scriptures to my writing because these are not my words, they are the inspired words of God that help to teach, instruct, and strengthen righteousness. When we read out loud, we are speaking words that impact the atmosphere. Satan knows this; therefore, he will always tempt us not to read. But reading is knowledge and understanding is power.

> But he answered and said, It is written, Man shall not live by bread alone, but by every word that proceedeth out of the mouth of God. (Matthew 4:4)

> When we speak of things of this nature, we are speaking the wisdom of God: But we speak the wisdom of God in a mystery, even the hidden wisdom, which God ordained before the world unto our glory: (1 Corinthians 2:6–7)

When we pray, the words we are speaking really have the power to change things. Prayer is exercising your faith to believe in what you are asking God for. This is why prayer is so important, not only in the workplace but in every area of life. Our faith should stretch beyond the boundaries and limitations that man has set for us. If we only believe, we can have. The Bible is all about having the faith to believe. If we do not believe, then where is our hope? How did it begin, and more so, where does it end? Our Father in heaven does not want us to be ignorant of the things concerning Him. In ancient times, the speech of man was the only method of sharing the wisdom of God; then God gave the scribes gifts to record the written Word. No matter how many variations of the Bible there is, God's Word and purpose will never change. He is still using the gifts of scribing today to bring people into the wisdom of who God created them to be. It is my prayer and hope that through my writing, the mind-set of the people will change to know that they can speak and move mountains (life situations) with their words, if only they believe.

> For verily I say unto you, that whosoever shall say unto this mountain, Be thou removed, and be thou cast into the sea; and shall not doubt in his heart, but shall believe that those things which he saith shall come to pass; he shall have whatsoever he saith. (Mark 11:23)

As the time to speak season pertains to the workplace, there is wisdom in knowing when to speak, especially when it involves other people. The workplace is attached to our purpose; hence we are accountable for our words. The enemy shows up in our workplace just like we do. The enemy's instructions are to release demonic activity as often as possible. They work through whomever they have access to. Their attributes are not limited to being an accuser or tempter; they also promote jealousy, envy, anger, hatred, to name just a few. When characteristics like these are in operation in the workplace, we know that evil is present. How we respond to those activities determines the working atmosphere. Even though we have the authority to speak, I believe that God's will is for us to filter. Just like when we pray His will be done, we are yielding to God's manifestation within His alignment. Spoken words can change our countenance, change our view and cause limitations in the process of our purpose.

The book of Proverbs highlights the wisdom of watching our speech:

> In the multitude of words there wanteth not sin: but he that refraineth his lips is wise. (Proverbs 10:19)

> He that keepeth his mouth keepeth his life: but he that openeth wide his lips shall have destruction. (Proverbs 13:3)

> Death and life are in the power of the tongue: and they that love it shall eat the fruit thereof. (Proverbs 18:21)

> In the mouth of the foolish is a rod of pride: but the lips of the wise shall preserve them. (Proverbs 14:3–13)

The season for us to speak is to take advantage of the appointed time to speak the promises and truth of what God has purposed for our lives. We have to welcome to move of God on our behalf. He will not go against your will. Speaking words of power at the appointed time takes our words into the atmosphere like a sphere. Our words can travel through time and hit God's intended target. God has given us permission to speak. When we are not aware of the power of our words, it is because we have been blinded to the truth of what is greater within us.

Situations and circumstances in our workplace can arise to shift us. Change comes when it is time for another season, whether that be for you or others. We should not despise change in the workplace. As long as the seasons are changing, then we are moving in our process. However, when we become stagnate for too long, we should seek God (Holy Spirit) for council. Not all changes will move you physically, or promote you into another position, but what they should do is expand your mind by giving you more wisdom, greater knowledge, and by enhancing your view of life. This confirms that you are progressing toward your purpose. Remember, everyone's purpose will not look the same, so do not compare or measure your purpose with others. Two people can have the same position in the workplace, but their footprint in life is totally different. As a result, the same change will impact them differently.

We all have an appointed time to speak. Take Moses and Aaron, for example. God had given Moses the instructions to speak to Pharaoh (King of Egypt) telling him to let the people go from that particular workplace. Moses was concerned about how his words would come across. God told him that He would make him (Moses) a god to Pharaoh, and Aaron a prophet. Sometimes there are people in our workplaces that can speak better than others. To some it is a gift to be able to speak profoundly. I've seen people who have that gift use it to their advantage because they are good with the flattering placement and flow of words. They can talk their way into something and back out at the same time, while the listener doesn't even know what has happened. Discern the spirit of these. Nevertheless, when God has an appointed time of you to speak, he has anointed those words. Moses was not released from the assignment because of his speaking impediment. He still had to speak to Pharaoh. Both Moses and Aaron spoke the words that God had given them for the king. God gives us assignments to speak, so accept them and speak well.

> And it came to pass on the day when the Lord spake unto Moses in the land of Egypt, That the Lord spake

unto Moses, saying, I am the Lord: speak thou unto Pharaoh king of Egypt all that I say unto thee. And Moses said before the Lord, Behold, I am of uncircumcised lips, and how shall Pharaoh hearken unto me?

And the Lord said unto Moses, See, I have made thee a god to Pharaoh: and Aaron thy brother shall be thy prophet. Thou shalt speak all that I command thee: and Aaron thy brother shall speak unto Pharaoh, that he send the children of Israel out of his land. And Moses and Aaron did as the Lord commanded them, so did they. (Exodus 6:28–30, 7:1–2, 6)

I will speak of thy testimonies also before kings, and will not be ashamed. (Psalm 119:46)

Prayer is a form of speaking. More so, it is powerful because we get the opportunity to talk (speak) directly with the Creator of heaven and earth through access via Christ (Ephesians 2; John 14:6). Intercession is just as important. When we pray on behalf of others, we are using our words to prophesy their future. Prayer is for the future. When we pray, we are asking for or referring to something in the future (i.e., to heal, set free, deliver, etc.). We are not praying to change anything in the past. Now, when we worship, we are speaking of the present/past/future time. Glorifying God for who He is (present) and praising Him for what He has done (past); and what our expectation is for what is to come (future). Keep praying concerning the workplace because it is needed so much in this time we are living in. More importantly, others need our prayers—those who love you and the ones who persecute you as well.

> But I say to you, love your enemies and pray for those who persecute you. (Matthew 5:44)

8: A time to love, and a time to hate; a time of war, and a time of peace

A Time to Love

Love is probably the strongest affection we have inwardly or outwardly. We can show that affection in a multitude of ways, customs, behaviors or even traditions. We all possess love within us. There are many words that can be compared to love, like crush, cherish, lust, yearning, adoration, idolatry, allegiance, longing, zeal, fondness, devotion, or passion. Love is held in high regards because of its strong characteristics that are often shown.

I believe that from the time we were formed in the womb we have all experienced love. When love is present, we may feel a strong affection for a person by way of a relationship. Some relationships are simply romantic or can be a strong physical desire for another person. We can also experience love for a family member or close friend. Another view of love is the way we feel about something we do, like loving to cook, play sports, do crafts, and so on.

> Beloved, let us love one another: for love is of God; and every one that loveth is born of God, and knoweth God. (1 John 4:7)

God is love. I personally think it is amazing how God created all of us in His image of love. His imagery is the purist of love. Our first commandment is to love. The second is to love our neighbor. I would say that love is the most important attribute of God we have. Everything created has an ingredient of love in it.

> Whoever does not love does not know God, because God is love. (1 John 4:8 NIV)

Love is active and living and it never dies no matter how we try to cover it up. How we sway our thoughts about someone or something may change, but love remains the same: it is strong and unbreakable. How many times have we heard a person say, "I don't love them anymore," or "I am not in love with them anymore"? Well this is not true. Love is a part of all mankind. Now, we may not like what a person does or our physical desires may change toward a person, but the love still exists. Many times, we want to equate love with our personal feelings. Our feelings are not love because love is much deeper than our feelings. We can feel one way on the surface any given day, then change and feel another way on the next day. That is not love. To truly examine love, we would need to study God because He is 100 percent love.

So many times, God has demonstrated His love to us, but there are many who are still blind to this. What if God said that He did not love us anymore, or that He was not in love with you any longer? Then He would not be representing who He is. The image of God is all love every day, all the time and forever, no matter what. As we know from the scriptures, the enemy blinded the minds of unbelievers so they won't see that Christ is the image of God.

> In whom the god of this world hath blinded the minds of them which believe not, lest the light of the glorious gospel of Christ, who is the image of God, should shine unto them. (2 Corinthians 4)

He even proved His love it by giving His only begotten Son so that we could have a chance at everlasting life. What other gift of love could be greater to receive? We are so focused at times on our immediate life here on earth that we do not take time to think about what is to come; but whether we want it to or not, it will come. We change, but love never does. We can never break God's original design, and that is to love God and one another.

This season to love is about an appointed time to demonstrate the love that God has placed within you. Many say they love, but how often do we take the time to demonstrate this love? Probably not often enough. A season to love as it pertains to the workplace is unique. I say this because normally there is such a lack of love shown in the workplace, especially toward Christ. Surprisingly, this is even true of workplaces such as churches! Working with one another will always have its challenges, but we are still required to love. We all know it can be hard to demonstrate the love of God at times. This is why I believe this season to love is so important.

> And now these three remain: faith, hope and love. But the greatest of these is love. (1 Corinthians 13:13 NIV)

We have covered many types of situations and circumstances that can occur in the workplace. Some can be heartbreaking or worse. When others do not demonstrate love toward us, we condemn them because we expect and want to be treated with love. When that does not happen, in most cases, we do not return love to them. There comes an appointed time when we are to exhibit the love that is within us. How you portray that love is between you and God. He will deal with you concerning love. Sometimes it may be a piercing of the heart, an act of kindness that will aid someone, or maybe a sacrifice to help others. God never promised that it would be easy to love, nevertheless I am sure it gets hard for God to love us too. I can see why this season should be an incremental part of our life, for if we do not exercise the love within us, how would others see or experience the love of God? He uses everything within us for His glory. God did not place love within us to be dormant. The workplace is where we come together to produce our fruit. Love is an essential fruit of the spirit. When we can work in love, the greater the fruit. Remember God said in Genesis, be fruitful and multiply:

> But the fruit of the Spirit is love, joy, peace, longsuffering, gentleness, goodness, faith. (Galatians 5:22)

When God created the heavens and earth, He had love in mind. Every living thing has their portion of love. Every human being, tree, plant, animal, even insect, demonstrates the love within them. Love is beautiful in all its splendor. You cannot physically touch love, but you can feel it. You cannot physically see love, but you know it exists. We can see the manifestation of love and that is a beautiful thing.

God and Jesus both often pointed out specific mandates concerning love. The commandments were given to Moses in love, and throughout the Bible, it talks about how most things point back to love. Obviously, love is important and plays an important role in life. This season is to point us to deeper love. It is easy to show love to those we like, but God wants us to have brotherly love as well. In the Bible, Romans 12:10 tells us to love one another with brotherly affection and with honor.

Our encounters in the workplace can sometimes be a love test. Have you ever worked in a place where there is a person who seems to be like a thorn sticking you from time to time? Have you had repeated instances when your patience and overflowing of love have become clogged? When you experience situations like this, most likely it is a love test. It is hard to love or feed people when they are sticking you. Jesus was good at teaching his disciples. He still taught them things even after he had risen from the dead. And now we are learning from his teaching. In John chapter 21, Jesus showed himself to the disciples after he rose from the dead. He asked Peter (Simon) three times if he loved him. Peter affirmed his love each time with yes. The first time Jesus responded, "feed my lambs," but the second and third time his response was, "feed my sheep." Both are considered his flock and are cherished (loved) by God. We are the flock. Why three times? Although Peter answered saying yes all three times, Jesus kept on asking the same question and Peter became grieved by the repeated questioning. We know how it is when someone asks us the same thing over again: we get frustrated, wanting to know why they keep asking. Obviously, there was a greater purpose as Jesus knew that Peter loved him. He wanted Peter to think about what it really means to love Him. To love Jesus is to love others as well. He wanted Peter to exercise that same love he has for Jesus to others by feeding them. This was Peter's work assignment. He was to demonstrate love by sharing the gospel of the kingdom of God.

> This is now the third time that Jesus shewed himself to his disciples, after that he was risen from the dead. So when they had dined, Jesus saith to Simon Peter, Simon, son of Jonas, lovest thou me more than these? He saith unto him, Yea, Lord; thou knowest that I love thee.
>
> He saith unto him, Feed my lambs. He saith to him again the second time, Simon, son of Jonas, lovest thou me? He saith unto him, Yea, Lord; thou knowest that I love thee.
>
> He saith unto him, Feed my sheep. He saith unto him the third time, Simon, son of Jonas, lovest thou me? Peter was grieved because he said unto him the third time, Lovest thou me? And he said unto him, Lord, thou knowest all things; thou knowest that I love thee. Jesus saith unto him, Feed my sheep. (John 21:14–17)

In Hebrew, the word ahab (aw-hab) or aheb (aw-hebe) means "to love." The verb is comparable to the English version, "to love," meaning "to have an emotional connection to, and desire either to possess or to be in the presence of the person or object." [50]The word refers to the love a man has for a woman or likewise a woman for a man. Love is not limited to just a man and woman. As mentioned above, there are various forms of the demonstrated love. The Bible describes love in a very compassionate way for us to understand. However, I think the most powerful words in 1 Corinthians 13 is that love never fails!

> Love is patient, love is kind. It does not envy, it does not boast, it is not proud. It does not dishonor others, it is not self-seeking, it is not easily angered, it keeps no record of wrongs. Love does not delight in evil but rejoices with the truth. It always protects, always trusts, always hopes, always perseveres. Love never fails. (1 Corinthians 13:4–8 NIV)

> Above all, love each other deeply, because love covers over a multitude of sins. (1 Peter 4:8 NIV)

A Time to Hate

Many view hate as an intense or extreme enmity toward someone or something. In Hebrew, it is called sane (saw-nay)—the primary root being "to hate" (personally). Sane can be classified as an intense emotion.[51] The word hatred is another form that can be used to refer to a person or things, including ideas, words, or objects. It can be referred to as an emotion of jealously. More so, hate can be considered as being set against something like a belief.

A season to hate can sound unreal since we know the power of love, which is the opposite of hate. In most cases, we direct hate at the enemy because of the hatred he has for us. Nevertheless, there is a time when we must hate the things that the enemy uses against us. King Solomon speaks about six things that the Lord hates in Proverbs 6. I do not believe that all things that God hates are included in this list: there are others, like having other gods, or worshipping graven images or objects, and others listed in the commandments. This information has been made known to us to that we can stride to be in alignment with righteousness.

> These six things doth the Lord hate: yea, seven are an abomination unto him: a proud look, a lying tongue, and hands that shed innocent blood, an heart that deviseth wicked imaginations, feet that be swift in running to mischief, a false witness that speaketh lies, and he that soweth discord among brethren. (Proverbs 6:15–19)

In most cases, we can find these types of abominations exist in the workplace. I believe that most of us have fallen into at least one of these categories. I also believe that we can never stop reviewing this list as a reminder of what God hates, and therefore, these are things we should hate also.

I want to spotlight a few of them to help us identify this season when it approaches. A lying tongue and a false witness that speak lies are closely connected. A lie is the opposite of the truth. Everything that God has created for us is based on truth. When a lie is present, it does not represent God at all. The Bible says that the devil is the father of lies.

> Ye are of your father the devil, and the lusts of your father ye will do. He was a murderer from the beginning, and abode not in the truth, because there is no truth in him. When he speaketh a lie, he speaketh of his own: for he is a liar, and the father of it. (John 8:44 KJV)

For if the Bible tells us what the support beam is for lies, and who is behind it, then we should want to be far from it. The season to hate is a reminder to stand for truth and what is good, pure and honest. The expectation for righteousness is the hold fast of the truth. We cannot grab a hold of a lie and run with it.

Surely, a false witness to a lie is viewed as a weak person and this is definitely not a characteristic of a good leader. How can we allow the enemy to trick us into such a dangerous web? In the workplace, I have seen this many times where management plot against an employee to cause them to fail. We see it happen, but we do nothing about it. Sometimes it is beyond our reach, but when it is not, and there is something we can do, still we do not act. To hate the enemy and the evil it represents is to stand with God. To hate evil is to expose the works of the enemy whenever possible. When we ignore and choose to be silent, it opens the door for it to happen to you. A season to hate is to take action so that God's glory and goodness can prevail. Choose truth over the lie, because the liars and others alike never win.

> But the fearful, and unbelieving, and the abominable, and murderers, and whoremongers, and sorcerers, and idolaters, and all liars, shall have their part in the lake which burneth with fire and brimstone: which is the second death. (Revelation 21:8)

Regarding feet that be swift in running to mischief—meaning trouble, misbehavior or intent to do damage—the driver behind a premeditated act can never be underestimated. Evil people go to great lengths to do wicked deeds against someone, and what is sad is that most of them do not truly understand the impact of evil. Those who rush off to perform an action that can harm someone else are missing a very important ingredient. Evil can drive many things. But the deadliest is the silent hate. Undermining and scheming to trip someone up is the work of the devil. The only way to beat evil is to hate evil. When we decide to surrender the world's way of living and accept Christ into our lives, we begin to hate what God hates. As long as we hate evil, it will not prevail against us.

In the workplace, there will be many opportunities to identify the works of the enemy. This is why we must pray for those we work with. It is so easy to come under the influence of evil. Have you ever worked with someone that did not like you? They may not have had a reason to dislike you, but they did anyway. It could be due to race, creed or other prejudices, all driven by evil. Conversely, you may have those people who like you but still wish to perform evil against you. Both are driven by evil.

We have to learn how to hate the evil and not the person. Remember, Satan will use whosoever to obtain access. Once access is granted, those times of evil trespassing can lead to bigger issues. There is something about hating evil that causes you to love more. Amazingly, we are stronger when we hate evil. The less room we have for evil, the more room we have to love. Evil opposes righteousness; it turns honesty into dishonest; it promotes darkness rather than light. Jesus is always our example. I honestly believe that Judas really liked Jesus, but because of his weakness for greed, it gave the enemy access to drive, which caused Judas to rush off to perform mischief. If Judas hated evil, then his weakness would not have won over him. Love will keep us in place.

Remember we cannot mistake love for lust. We can always identify lust because it is temporary. As we hate evil, be careful not to perform wickedness toward the hate, else we become like the evil. So, when the season to hate presents itself, be ready and armed with the fullest of love to expose and disarm it. We are reminded that our amour is in the Word. The more we read and study the Bible, the more we become full of love.

A Time of War

War can be a state or period of fighting against one another in a confrontational form. Some have a theory that says that the root of almost all of our wars is religion, even in recent years; even political wars can have a religious root. Some men and women have a greater allegiance to their country and its beliefs than their own personal relationship with God. Some wars are driven by territorial increase of land, power, greed, economic benefits, personages/properties or terrorism; all of which can have a spiritual impact on a nation, state, city, community, or our way of living.

> Then there are some battles that are not at all about gaining something tangible from the battle. Many times, warriors have walked away without anything in their hands but respect and honor. Some would marvel at this, but King Saul learned this the hard way (see 1 Samuel 15).

The results of some wars can be bloodshed, hostility or rivalry. The Bible talks about war being a significant part of the lives of the people in the Old Testament. Military experience was a known expectation and skill for many men and women. In those days, war could happen at any given moment, as most men were expected to fight without rebuttal. The risk of survival was high, nevertheless it was a part of who God created them to be—it was their purpose. This way of thinking has changed a lot over the years.

The Hebrew word for war is milehamah (mil-khaw-maw), and it means "battle." When individuals went into battle, it was to gain more land or territory or other resources.[52] At times, it was because they were attacked for power struggles.

Depending on the outcome, some were taken into captivity. This form of war can still happen today.

Normally, in the United States, a declaration of war is made by the government (president or national leader) especially when it is between a state and nation. Generally, this is the process, but by law the president can deploy troops with or without a formal declaration for a period of time. When someone engages in war, the place of battle becomes their workplace for that season. When war is at hand, an individual's purpose has risen to its highest point because their life is on the line. The enemy you fight against is your adversary and you must do whatever it takes to survive.

Our history tells of many seasons of terrible wars that resulted in the loss of countless lives. Nevertheless, God ordains war. The first mention of war in the Bible can be found in Genesis 14. Good and evil plays a factor in most wars; from the fall of Adam all the way to Jesus, and even now, wars are still a battle between good and evil. The Bible portrays God as being faithful in punishing evil, but also faithful in His love for us, especially for those who love Him and follow His commands.

> When thou goest out to battle against thine enemies, and seest horses, and chariots, and a people more than thou, be not afraid of them: for the Lord thy God is with thee…And shall say unto them, Hear, O Israel, ye approach this day unto battle against your enemies: let not your hearts faint, fear not, and do not tremble, neither be ye terrified because of them; For the Lord your God is he that goeth with you, to fight for you against your enemies, to save you. (Deuteronomy 20:1, 3–4)

War seasons comes in difference facets. Some wars will consist of a physical battleground with multitudes of people. However, some wars can wage with no limitations to the number of people impacted in a particular battle. A battle can be between just two people; number has never been a factor with God. He can use one or one-hundred million for a purpose, denoting that God, our Father in heaven is sovereign in every way.

When someone enters into a season for war it is an opportune time to stand for what you believe in. Going into battle does not always mean having a host with you. In fact, it can be quite lonely at times because you may not have someone to help share in your distress or the debris from the battle. Fighting for your cause can sometimes take you down a long road of combat, depending on the origin of the war. The thing about war is you never know how it is going to end. Faith plays a major role in any battle. This refers to believers as well as nonbelievers. Everyone believes in something, whether they proclaim it is in God or not. Even a nonbeliever will cry out to someone higher than themselves when the pressure is at its highest point.

War has the potential to transform a person. Many veterans today tell how the experience of war left them in a totally different capacity. Some were physically changed, but many were mentally changed as a result of war. A battle always seeks to change something. The outcome of a war will always be significant to those who have gone through the battle. What most people do not realize is wars happen more often than they think: the majority do not recognize a war until they are in it.

God uses war for different reasons. We are living in a time when it is important to increase our understanding of war. The intent of war is not always to physically kill. War can bring much positivity. Sometimes it will bring evolution, meaning development, growth or maturation, progression or even transformation. A season for war in the workplace takes on a challenge for change. In most cases, war comes for the advancement of good prevailing over evil. Waging war in the workplace has become more common especially from an evil root. We must remember that evil is ever present when trying to do well.

War can come from an enemy when threatened, and will therefore invoke us to act against them. We have probably seen wars start in the workplace when one experiences a threat from another, stemming from a role change. I believe we have all acted as though we are (or at least entertained the thought of being) better than others, wanting more power, and seizing the opportunity to shine over our coworkers or laborers. Sometimes we are more conscience of it than others. Have we not forgotten that God created us in his image? It is in us to have dominion. Ruling was given to us by God (Genesis 1:26, 28). We just need to operate in the principal of love and wisdom of good and evil to govern it so we do not fall in self-destruction.

Evil can be like a fire, spreading rapidly to consume anything in its path. This is seen at times when the spirit of pride is present. Pride is vainglory. This is what happened to Lucifer (whom God created) and it led him to destruction. Some other characteristics can be arrogance, boastfulness, overconfidence, or having a self-importance or swagger about oneself. These are types of spirits that act as fuel to always wanting more power. This not only happened to Lucifer, but Jezebel, and certain kings. Apostle Paul talked about the issue with pride with the Gentile Christians and unbelieving Jews. So, you see pride can arise in both righteous and unrighteous people, but God still hates it.

> Better is the end of a thing than the beginning thereof: and the patient in spirit is better than the proud in spirit. (Ecclesiastes 7:8)

> The fear of the Lord is to hate evil: pride, and arrogancy, and the evil way, and the froward mouth, do I hate. (Proverbs 8:13)

> Let nothing be done through strife or vainglory;but in lowliness of mind let each esteem other better than themselves. (Philippians 2:3)

As mentioned before, the workplace can include the church also. Some people have working roles in the church. It is hard to believe that the spirit of pride should exist there, but it does. Authority and positions can sometimes bring out the worst in people. Pride creeps in slowly through the cracks until it can gain its strength. Once it is full blown, it heads for destruction. Sometimes pride wars against itself: spirit versus flesh. The church is no exception to the rule, as titles and position are earth bound. Now we still have to respect and heed those in authority or positions in the church, as well as any given workplace. Yet, we are still accountable for what they do while holding any position here on earth.

The body of Christ definitely has room for more understanding concerning the mysteries and secret things of God. Pride is only one spirit that can invoke war. There are many others, which are not known to some. Pride can give an impression of knowing it all. Howbeit, we can even think we know it all? It is necessary to seek the things of God to understand warfare. Jeremiah is one biblical reference that tells us God wants to show us mighty things we do not know.

> Call to Me, and I will answer you, and show you great and mighty things, which you do not know. (Jeremiah 33:3)

From my experience, pride and control are very closely knitted together. Both are often seen operating together, especially in war times. Warfare brings on a different mind-set because of the defense mechanism that exists within all us. How we respond during war times is key to the outcome and survival of the war. Many churches cannot even work or worship together because of these two war-centric spirits: pride and control. They can both cause tremendous damage and injury in the church from a spiritual perspective. Sometimes the injury can be so deeply rooted that some never recover. My opinion is, why would anyone in their "right mind" want to wage war within the church unless it is driven by Satan himself? Nonetheless, we see it every day on social media, the news, even down to our individual local churches. It is a silent killer, hiding behind things like ideologies, philosophies, religious systems and nonbiblical church cultures.

It is important to remember that all war has a spiritual foundation. War starts in the spirit and mind before it is ever fought physically on the ground. Some may fight it in the flesh, but the source is spiritual. The season for war is ranked from a much larger capacity. It is a direct hit from principalities, powers, spiritual wickedness, and ruler of the darkness no matter what branch or foundation it stems from.

> For we wrestle not against flesh and blood, but against principalities, against powers, against the rulers of the darkness of this world, against spiritual wickedness in high places. (Ephesians 6:12)

> For the weapons of our warfare are not carnal but mighty in God for pulling down strongholds (2 Corinthians 10:4 NKJV)

War toward the church will remain spiritual. Some seasons of war are greater than others. A war commander or leader should have spiritual and prophetic insight, strong prayer relationship (intercessor), and seek godly wisdom and council before and during the spiritual battle, especially for the church. In addition, the Bible calls out specific armor to help withstand battle against the enemy. This should be our daily gear in preparation for the season of war at any given time.

> Wherefore take unto you the whole armour of God, that ye may be able to withstand in the evil day, and having done all, to stand.
>
> Stand therefore, having your loins girt about with truth, and having on the breastplate of righteousness; And your feet shod with the preparation of the gospel of peace;
>
> Above all, taking the shield of faith, wherewith ye shall be able to quench all the fiery darts of the wicked. And take the helmet of salvation, and the sword of the Spirit, which is the word of God:

> Praying always with all prayer and supplication in the Spirit, and watching there unto with all perseverance and supplication for all saints; (Ephesians 6:13)

A Time of Peace

To have peace is a wonderful thing. Peace usually precedes something. Like after a war ends, there can be a state of concord, tranquility that follows. Proceeding the passing of a storm there is usually a sense of peace in the atmosphere. When restitution is given to restore, there lies a peace. Thinking on the things that brings a season of peace these questions come to mind:

- Who is the author of peace?
- How do we identify peace?
- What does a season of peace bring?

There are scriptures that point to true peace being of God. Peace comes in seasons or at appointed times. Peace is known as one of the fruits of the spirit. At times there is a desperate cry for peace, but it is not always found. We can sense and obtain peace in our mind, heart or spirit but God is the giver of peace.

Who can thoroughly understand the depths of peace? The peace of God is said to be past or beyond our understanding. We cannot totally understand the origin of peace, as God is the author. He is referred to below as the God of peace.

And the God of peace shall bruise Satan under your feet shortly. The grace of our Lord Jesus Christ be with you. Amen. (Romans 16:20)

Those things, which ye have both learned, and received, and heard, and seen in me, do: and the God of peace shall be with you. (Philippians 4:9)

But the fruit of the Spirit is love, joy, peace, longsuffering, gentleness, goodness, faith, (Galatians 5:22)

Peace is one of those revealed seasons or appointed times in our lives. Many have searched for peace in their own strength but are not successful. God's thoughts are not as ours, and we cannot begin to really comprehend the depths of Him. He gives us understanding by way of revelation. The revelation brings a light that cannot be measured by man. We know peace and can recognize it when it is revealed, but we cannot compute, estimate or mark it when it starts or ends.

But as it is written, Eye hath not seen, nor ear heard, neither have entered into the heart of man, the things which God hath prepared for them that love him. But God hath revealed them unto us by his Spirit: for the Spirit searcheth all things, yea, the deep things of God. (1 Corinthians 2:9–10)

Even in our work life, a season of peace comes to bring harmony, calmness, freedom or a release; sometimes healing and restoration too. Peace can promote encouragement and restful understanding. This can also be a season to set your mind at ease and find quiet or tranquility. Also, this season can bring a relationship in harmony and wholeness, rather than being in a state of strife and war. Love is seen in peace. The word peace has power. Even when reading or speaking of peace, it can become activated at that moment.

And the peace of God, which passeth all understanding, shall keep your hearts and minds through Christ Jesus. (Philippians 4:7)

When peace is present, our spirit is comforted. The status of peace can be a state of resting, calmness or a feeling of being at ease in our spirit, mind, and soul. Be aware that anger, fear, rage, and torment are opposites of peace. When these opposites are active, there is a great lack of peace.

Shalom (shaw-lone`) means "peace" in Hebrew; it can also be defined as "welfare, health, prosperity." In the noun form, it means completeness. Shalom can have the sense of tranquility, at ease, or being unconcerned. [53] The term Jehovah Shalom is used in the Bible in Judges 6:24, where Gideon built an altar and named it to reference God as being peace.

The Angel of the Lord had already spoken to Gideon, letting him know that Jehovah was speaking to him and would be with him (Judges 6:16). Once Gideon perceived that God was actually speaking to him, he feared death because it was known that a person could not see the face of God alive (Exodus 33:20). Gideon like many, felt stressed and fearful, needing the peace of God for comfort. In Gideon's case, as peace was spoken and fear was removed, he was able to rest, knowing that he was not going to die. Here you see that peace banishes fear, as the two cannot dwell together.

> And when Gideon perceived that he was an angel of the Lord, Gideon said, Alas, O Lord God! for because I have seen an angel of the Lord face-to-face. And the Lord said unto him, Peace be unto thee; fear not: thou shalt not die. Then Gideon built an altar there unto the Lord, and called it Jehovahshalom. (Judges 6:22–24)

Have you ever worked in a hostile environment where the stress level had risen out of control? When these types of work conditions are active, prayer is needed immediately to disarm the enemy in your surroundings. Stress only leads to more distress and access to other doors. Prayer changes things. This is not just a cliché of words. Prayer and speaking the scriptures raise a standard against the adversary's motives and tactics. The enemy's goal is to invoke fear whenever possible. Fear attacks our mind and thoughts, therefore making us weak. Hostile working environments are open ground for fear if we allow them to be. Working under the pressure of fear of losing a job, your position, how much you get paid, or of being threatened or bullied in the workplace can all cause us to react with an unsound mind. This is never good and will not bring wholesome results. Peace is the remedy for fear. When this happens, pray for peace. Speak peace over your workplace. Pray for the person who is provoking the fear. God sees things that we cannot. Keep in mind He sets the seasons and times for both war and peace.

As mentioned before, at the end there is peace. When there is a shift in the workplace, especially when the assignment is coming to an end, there will be peace. To successfully prepare for the next season, we should seek to have peace in crossing over to our new season. Even as I write about the last season mentioned in Ecclesiastes, I sense a peace in my spirit. Reflecting back on writing about each one of the seasons, there was such a deeper view because they each had different challenges and perspectives. To make it to the end of the twenty-eight seasons called out, I found the peace and serenity of each one. Great is the understanding that at the end of each season, there is peace. From a prophetic view, I can see why Solomon placed it last. Peace comes at the end.

> But the Comforter, which is the Holy Ghost, whom the Father will send in my name, he shall teach you all things, and bring all things to your remembrance, whatsoever I have said unto you. Peace I leave with you, my peace I give unto you: not as the world giveth, give I unto you. Let not your heart be troubled, neither let it be afraid. (John 14:26–27)

Bringing closure to a season is like having a Comforter to aid with the transition. Remember: do not be afraid nor let your heart be troubled by changes of season, but know that God is with you. Apostle Paul often closes his conversation with a peace declaration. Although the benediction is given at times, it is not the end. The words are a continuation.

Now the Lord of peace himself give you peace always by all means. The Lord be with you all. (2 Thessalonians 3:16)

Now the God of peace be with you all. Amen. (Romans 15:33)

A Season Spent on an Island

By far, the book of Revelation is the most enduring and unveiling book in the Bible. This book was written by one of the twelve disciples named John. He was also referred to as the apostle John, and identified in the book of John 13:23 as the one whom Jesus loved. He experienced and wrote about one of the most captivating experiences in the Bible.

John endured a great season while being on the island of Patmos. I want to share this particular event from a purpose-driven perspective. I believe that it will help to encourage those who go through a life change for a season.

A major shift in John's life started when he was exiled or banished from his workplace in Ephesus (Rome), where he led a powerful ministry teaching about the gospel of the kingdom. In reading about John's background before his exile, it appears that his workplace had become a heated environment because of his teaching. Sometimes the heat is an indication that a fire is underway.

We can assume that his banishment or separation from his family, friends, and environment came unexpectedly. That is how fast a season can occur. We can only imagine the hardship he experienced at being placed on the island without choice. John had no idea what God was up to. Sometimes it is hard to wrap our mind around things that shift our entire life.

When your workplace shifts, everything in your life shifts in spirit. The workplace has spiritual ties because it is tied to your purpose. Just a reminder: your workplace is where you spend most of your waking time, and it can come in many different physical manifestations, but each workplace is part of your life assignment.

So for John, when the shift happened, a new season began. We can only speculate how long he was on the island before the great encounters began and how long they lasted before he could record them. The Bible simply says that he was in the spirit on the Lord's day.

> I was in the Spirit on the Lord's day, and heard behind me a great voice, as of a trumpet. (Revelation 1:10)

When God places us in a season, especially to be used, it is outside of our personal timeline of planning. Especially when there is an environment (workplace) change. Every separation is unique and not considered to be a cookie-cutter, meaning the parting process is never the same when it occurs.

In John's case, his purpose was so instrumental to a great awakening to the world, that the solitude was key. The environment had to be prepared by God for the purposed work to be done. The place could be considered as:

- A place conducive to absolute intimacy;
- The right atmosphere with no hindrances from others;
- Isolation so that hearing cannot be impaired;
- The perfect light to see His glory;
- A place where trust in God is the only alternative;

Patmos was the chosen geographical place in order to give the hidden piece of knowledge of the end times to the world. In addition, John received a global message to the churches, which are still relevant today. I want you to understand the importance of John's season on this island, not only for the great message but also to note the global influence and power the season produced. This will help many in recognizing the value when we go through a season.

The season that John spent on Patmos was definitely an appointed time by God. This was a season of great change for him. He was already known as a good apostle, but I believe that after this encounter, he answered his true calling as a prophet of God. Prophets not only see into the future, but they are charged to foretell it at an appointed time. When you come out of seasons such as this, there is no doubt about who God called you to be:

- Those He calls, He equips for the work;
- Those He calls, He makes room for the gift;
- Those He calls, He sends out to do the work;
- Those He calls, He anoints with power.

It is unknown to me how long John was on the island, but like all seasons, the start and end timeline are not as important as what was encountered during the season. The island of Patmos became John's new workplace. From a geographical perspective, Patmos was a small, barren and rugged island. Located on the Aegean Sea near the coast of Asia Minor; which is present-day Turkey. His day-to-day living conditions were not mentioned in the Bible, but we can only imagine it was difficult.

Revelation 1:1–2 tells us that Jesus sent an angel to John who testifies to everything he saw. He gave him a futuristic vision of the dreadful gloom that is to come. To absorb the graphical imagery and the testimony of Jesus that offers us hope had to be one of the most captivating visions ever experienced and written by man. What other book can compare to the book of Revelation? The experience John had was not only captivating, but the messages within the book are multifaceted with the greatest impact to mankind. He was chosen to experience a season of great oracles.

To see such an extraordinary vision had to be mind-blowing in itself. Then God used his divinatory gift to write the book so the whole world would know the truth about Jesus and our future. Although John clearly heard the voice of Christ in the vision (Revelation 1:10), the Holy Spirit was fully activated throughout the process as John recorded. The images in the vision were indescribable, so the Holy Spirit helped John portray what they were like for better understanding. Who else could illuminate the revelation of God's word but the Holy Spirit?

> But God hath revealed them unto us by Spirit: for the Spirit searcheth all things, yea, the deep things of God. For what man knoweth the things of a man, save the spirit of man which is in him? even so the things of God knoweth no man, but the Spirit of God. Now we have received, not the spirit of the world, but the spirit which is of God; that we might know the things that are freely given to us of God. Which things also we speak, not in the words which man's wisdom teacheth,but which the Holy Ghost teacheth;comparing spiritual things with spiritual. (1 Corinthians 2:10–16)

As an inspired writer, I can certainly relate the spiritual things of God. In my writing, I must rely on the Holy Spirit to help expound on what God reveals to me. Many times, I have to wait and tarry for the Holy Spirit to reveal; but I don't mind waiting. It is important to me that what I write points directly to His light.

John's writing style in the book of Revelation is quite different from his other writings because he experienced a major shift (season) in his life. What John witnessed was so remarkable, and was destined to be shared throughout generations. The book is exceptionally anointed as it describes the art of future events and the hidden knowledge known to man.

There is so much in the revelatory message behind the experience. We could say that John wrote in a very specific genre as a result of his season in Patmos. This writing was distinctive because it was written in great depth, concerning the end of the world, in addition to God's judgments. His inspired apocalyptic (apoc-a-lyp-tic) warnings of disaster, following the signs, come unrestrained as only can be given in the spirit. Although John was a strong man of God, who witnessed and walked with Jesus, I am sure this seasonal journey was very challenging.

In some form or fashion, many of us have experienced a Patmos type of change where God separated us from an existing environment for a season. In some cases, our separation place may have become a condition that prevented us from moving to our next level. Most times, when seasons enter our lives, we have not planned for them. The result can be a breaking-away of our normal surroundings.

There was a season in my life where I experienced a jagged, rocky, testing place in my life. It seemed as though it happened overnight. Suddenly I was shifted into this place of solitude. There was a huge void in my life where the emptiness seemed to have no end. Others tried to reach me, but I could not connect because the spiritual distance was too great. I spent days weeping and not understanding how my life had deviated to such a downward spiral, and could not escape. What I did find by being in this place was that loneliness has a vein that feeds insecurity. It lures you to believe that you are not worthy and that God has forgotten you. This appointed time was invoked by God. Sometimes God just wants you to Himself. He wants to restore what has been broken, mend your torn spirit, and build you up to carry forth a blessing. Our Patmos is not a bad place, but it is a resting place where you refine yourself. The strength and wisdom you gain in solitude with God is to prepare you for kingdom work.

After a while, God began to speak to me. First, He took me back in time when the shift first happened and showed me the signs, indicators, and flags that I had ignored beforehand. The intent of the warnings was to prepare me so that when the shift happened, I would be ready. Many times we stay wrapped in our emotions, not realizing that God does not operate in our emotions; therefore, the process of reaching a spiritual state in which we can hear God is delayed.

During my Patmos period, I learned so much more about God, our Father in heaven. My prayer life became much stronger. I was eager to read more of the Bible and other books to draw closer to Him. Every tear of sadness, every fear, and every feeling of emptiness turned into a yearning for more of Him. The Holy Spirit revealed some amazing things to me that changed my life and relationship with Him forever. It was after this season I began writing, and my prophetic gift was revealed.

When God places you in a season that appears to be of solitude (your personal Patmos), please know that the process within that season is for a greater purpose. As mentioned, some of us have experienced those times when we have been set apart from our environment or what's known as the familiar place in our life. Each separation process is different. We all have our own footprint in life, and our purpose and outcome are unique to us.

The initial shock of feeling uprooted and separated (in Patmos) can take us on an emotional ride, and feel traumatic for some, before there is a spiritual calming. Like Apostle John, we will find that we are not in the journey alone. It is written that the Lord God will never leave or forsake you (Hebrew 13:5). It is wise to let God be our first alternative to reach for.

Peace and instruction awaits those who seek Him. I encourage you to find the calm resolve and allow the Holy Spirit to reveal the works of God operating in your life. Understanding the workplaces and the fact that we are laborers is key to our assignments here on the earth. Like the seasons, as they change, we change too. Our workplaces will come and go, but our divine purpose remains the same.

CHAPTER 5

PRAYERS FOR THE WORKPLACE

CHAPTER 5

PRAYERS FOR THE WORKPLACE

Thanking God for Our Workplace

Our Father in heaven, we thank you for another day you have given us to live. We praise you for everything you have done, everything we have, and all you are going to do in our lives. We are so grateful that we have a mighty God that loves and cares for us. Your love is continually revealed through the resurrection of your Son Jesus, and we thank you for your Holy Spirit.

We thank you for the workplace you have given us. Continue to give us our daily bread as we fulfill our destiny here on earth. Give us greater understanding concerning our purpose and the plan you designed for us. Reveal our spiritual vision to see you knitting everything together for our good. Open our hearts to receive the spiritual impartations as it pertains to our workplace.

Father, open our ears to hear and receive the truth regarding our purpose. Teach us how to count every blessing. Build us up, and strengthen us to finish our purpose in life. We are so grateful that our true reward comes from you.

- Father, we thank you for every job and assignment you have blessed us with.

- We thank you for every open door you have sent us through;
- We thank you for every person we have come in contact with in the workplace;
- We thank you for the opportunity to work for you;
- We thank you for teaching us to use our gifts in the workplace;
- We thank you for entrusting us to do your will;
- We thank you for the induced labor that gives birth to our purpose;
- We thank you for every season you have given us in the workplace;
- We thank you for using the workplace for your glory;
- We thank you for continued grace and mercies you show us every day.

Father, the workplace is such a blessing, and we thank you for the opportunity to be used to bless others through our assignment in the workplace. Protect our workplaces and the people you have assigned to be there. May there be peace always in our workplace. In Jesus's name. Amen.

Prayer for Our Leaders in the Workplace

Our Father in heaven, we praise and honor you. You are the Creator of heaven and earth. We take time to worship you, and thank you for loving us. Thank you for your inspired Word written that unveils our history and truth about you. You are the "Greatest Leader" of all. Continue to reveal your glory daily.

We thank you for creating leaders. The role of a leader was designed by you. Open our understanding to greater insight about the levels you have for us. Give us wisdom and greater discernment of your qualifications of being a successful leader. Fill the leaders all over this world with your spirit to lead your people. Let them have spiritual vision to see beyond the physical surface. Equip them with your tools and armor to defeat the enemy when he comes. Strengthen them to lead in righteousness.

Teach the leaders to truly understand the meaning of team building. Give them a vision of one in heart, mind, and spirit. Let them see their assignment of purpose. Our prayer is that every leader fulfills their God-given assignment.

Father, we pray for all leaders in the workplace;

- We pray that leaders have greater understanding of their divine purpose and assignment in the workplace;
- We pray that the love of God and Christ live in their hearts;
- We pray that you, our Father in heaven, will guide and lead them as they lead others;
- We pray that leaders will increase in wisdom and knowledge concerning spiritual things;

- We pray for the equipping of our leaders so that they may be able to train and build up others;
- We pray for increase in their lives to be a blessing to others;
- We pray for their process and preparation for passing the baton on to future leaders;
- We pray that every leader has a spiritual relationship and prayer life with you;
- We pray that leaders seek you, Father, first, for direction and instruction on how to lead your people successfully; and
- We pray for the protection and safety of our leaders in and outside of the workplace.

Father, bless their families and homes where they dwell. Increase them and enlarge their territories that they be great in your sight as your will unfolds in their lives. Bless them going in and going out that they may be a greater blessing to your people.

Most of all, Father, give us a heart to always pray for our leaders! In Jesus's name. Amen.

Prayer for Wrestling with Our Purpose

Our Father in heaven, we love you. You are the Alpha and Omega, the beginning and the end. You are the author and finisher of faith. We are so grateful and filled with alteration and compassion for the will you have for our lives.

Father, you are so good to us. You have divinely favored us to have a workplace here on earth. We are nothing without you. We are so glad that you have purposed our lives long before we were born. You never cease to amaze us in your works.

Help us to understand more about you and how our lives are mapped to your plan. Your purpose is universal, and all who live are impacted.

Father, help us not to wrestle against our purpose and plan you have for us.

- Help us to see your vision for our life.
- Give us the patience to wait in greater expectation of your will.
- Help us to understand your timeline for our life, and not to push "our will."
- Let us reflect on your how your yoke is easy, and how your burden is light.
- Give us the wisdom to prepare for our next level in you.
- Father, give us spiritual insight to discern the killers of our purpose.
- Let us follow your will to prevent delay of our purpose.
- Help us to stay focused and not war against your will for us.
- Teach us to wait on you.

- Give us wisdom in choosing our battles.
- Let us be comforted in knowing that you are working everything for our good.
- Forgive us, Father, when we wrestle against your purpose and plan for us.

Father, give us understanding that the challenges are there to strengthen us and not to war against. We thank you for the journey, and the finished product we will become. In Jesus's name. Amen.

Prayer to Help Us Through Our Seasons

Our Father in heaven, but not far away. You are beautiful in all of your splendor. In you, there is the fullness of righteousness, wisdom, goodness, and peace. We thank you for the seasons within our workplaces.

Father, your timing is perfect. You are the Creator of seasons. It is you who gives the appointed times to our purpose-driven life. The beginning and the end is established by you. We are so thankful to be a part of your will. Your love is everlasting, not seasonal.

Clearly, you demonstrate your love through every season we go through. We thank you that seasons mark the changes or events in our lives. Those marks "tell the time" directed at our purpose:

- Reveal to us each season you take us through in the workplace;
- Give us a greater understanding when a season ends, and another begins;
- Help us to grow within each work assignment you give us;
- Let each season reveal its purpose and how to win within the process;
- Give us clarity for direction and guidance within our season;
- Help us to use sound judgment while in our seasons;
- Let us be in complete harmony with your will for our lives;
- Holy Spirit we invite you to be fully activated in every season;

- Give us more wisdom in our season so we won't rely on our own intellect;
- Continue to expose the enemy when he comes to steal, kill and destroy;
- Let each interval through the seasons bring an increase in our spiritual walk;
- Train us up in the way we should go in each season of our lives; and
- Let the revelation of each season bring an abundance in our lives.

Father, we are so thankful for your mercy and how it endures forever. Thank you for the seasons that cause us to mature, so we can be evaluated to the next level toward our purpose. We thank you for your grace in each season. Most of all, Father, thank you for imparting seasons into our purpose. In Jesus's name. Amen.

Praying for One Another in the Workplace

Our Father in heaven, your love is so powerful. Jesus is the perfect example of your love. To show us how much you love us, you sent your Son to die for our sins. That is a profound validation of the greatest love.

Teach us how to love like Christ loved the church. Show us how we are all connected to one source and that is You. Our heart was created to hold all the love we could ever imagine. Love is anointed to share with others.

Father, show us how to see and love a person from your view;

- Let our hearts be filled with the love of Christ for those within our workplaces;
- We pray for godlier friendships within our workplaces;
- We pray that those in the workplace embrace righteousness;
- Teach us how to love thy enemies and neighbor as thyself;
- Train us to be patient with those in the workplaces;
- Father, keep reminding us that love never fails;
- We pray that you give them the desires of their heart;
- Father, teach us to forgive quickly when a trespass has been made against us;
- We pray that their eyes be open to spiritual things;
- We pray that they be healed in their mind, body, and spirit;
- We pray that those in the workplace surrender to God's purpose for their lives;
- We continue to pray for their assignment in the workplace;

- Help keep us from evil so we will not afflict pain;
- Teach us to love one another more as we press forward in our purpose.

Father, you have placed us in the workplace to not only fulfill our purpose, but to love and pray for others. It is our prayer that your will be done in the lives of every person we come in contact with in the workplace. Thank you for bringing new people to our lives in the workplace. Let your will be done that I might be a blessing to them within the assigned season. In Jesus's name. Amen.

Greater love hath no man than this, that a man lay down his life for his friends. (John 15:13)

NOTES

Chapter 3. WRESTLING WITH PURPOSE

1. Mlakah—Hebrew meaning: James Strong, The New Strong's Expanded Exhaustive Concordance of the Bible (Thomas Nelson, 2010) 4399.

2. Merriam-Webster Online, s.v. "prepare," accessed November 18, 2017, http://www.merriam-webster.com/dictionary/prepare.

3. Merriam-Webster Online, s.v. "pain," accessed November 15, 2017, http://www.merriam-webster.com/dictionary/pain.

Chapter 4. SEASONS TELL TIME

4. Season: Paula Price, The Prophet's Dictionary, Revised and Expanded Edition. ed. (US: Whitaker House, 2007) 492.

5. Merriam-Webster Online, LearnersDictionary.com, s.v. "born," http://www.learnersdictionary.com/definition/born.

6. Merriam-Webster Online, s.v. "born," https://www.merriam-webster.com/dictionary/born.

7. Yalad—Hebrew meaning: James Strong, The New Strong's Expanded Exhaustive Concordance of the Bible (Thomas Nelson, 2010) 3205.

8. Nata mlakah—Hebrew meaning: James Strong, The New Strong's Expanded Exhaustive Concordance of the Bible (Thomas Nelson, 2010) 5193.

9. Aqar—Hebrew meaning: James Strong, The New Strong's Expanded Exhaustive Concordance of the Bible (Thomas Nelson, 2010) 6131.

10. Merriam-Webster Online, s.v. "pluck," accessed November 23, 2017 https://www.merriam-webster.com/dictionary/pluck.

11. Merriam-Webster Online, s.v. "kill," accessed October 13, 2017, http://www.merriam-webster.com/dictionary/kill.

12. Raphah—Hebrew meaning: James Strong, The New Strong's Expanded Exhaustive Concordance of the Bible (Thomas Nelson, 2010) 7495.

13. Merriam-Webster Online, s.v. "breakdown," accessed November 20, 2017, https://www.merriam-webster.com/dictionary/break%20down

14. Parats—Hebrew meaning: James Strong, The New Strong's Expanded Exhaustive Concordance of the Bible (Thomas Nelson, 2010) 6555.

15. Mizbeach—Hebrew meaning: James Strong, The New Strong's Expanded Exhaustive Concordance of the Bible (Thomas Nelson, 2010) 4196.

16. Banah—Hebrew meaning: James Strong, The New Strong's Expanded Exhaustive Concordance of the Bible (Thomas Nelson, 2010) 1129.

17. Merriam-Webster Online, s.v. "up," accessed November 24, 1017, https://www.merriam-webster.com/dictionary/up.

18. Petros—Greek meaning: James Strong, The New Strong's Expanded Exhaustive Concordance of the Bible (Thomas Nelson, 2010) 4074.

19. Petra—Greek meaning: James Strong, The New Strong's Expanded Exhaustive Concordance of the Bible (Thomas Nelson, 2010) 4073.

20. Ekklesia—Greek meaning: James Strong, The New Strong's Expanded Exhaustive Concordance of the Bible (Thomas Nelson, 2010) 1577.

21. Bakah—Hebrew meaning: James Strong, The New Strong's Expanded Exhaustive Concordance of the Bible (Thomas Nelson, 2010) 1058.

22. Klaio—Greek meaning: James Strong, The New Strong's Expanded Exhaustive Concordance of the Bible (Thomas Nelson, 2010) 2799.

23. Merriam-Webster Online, s.v. "laugh," accessed November 22, 2017, https://www.merriam-webster.com/dictionary/laugh.

24. Sachaq—Hebrew meaning: James Strong, The New Strong's Expanded Exhaustive Concordance of the Bible (Thomas Nelson, 2010) 7832.

25. Merriam-Webster Online, s.v. "dance," accessed November 24, 2017, https://www.merriam-webster.com/dictionary/dance.

26. Raqad—Hebrew meaning: James Strong, The New Strong's Expanded Exhaustive Concordance of the Bible (Thomas Nelson, 2010) 7540.

27. Commentary on Isaiah 13:21, http://www.godvine.com/bible/isaiah/13–21.

28. Bible Study Tools, s.v. "satyr," http://www.biblestudytools.com/dictionaries/eastons-bible-dictionary/satyr.html.

29. Merriam-Webster Online, s.v. "scatter," accessed November 20, 2017, https://www.merriam-webster.com/dictionary/scatter.

30. Eben—Hebrew meaning: James Strong, The New Strong's Expanded Exhaustive Concordance of the Bible (Thomas Nelson, 2010) 68.

31. Kanac—Hebrew meaning: James Strong, The New Strong's Expanded Exhaustive Concordance of the Bible (Thomas Nelson, 2010) 3664.

32. Merriam-Webster Online, s.v. "embrace, accessed November 16, 2017, https://www.merriam-webster.com/dictionary/embrace.

33. Chabaq—Hebrew meaning: James Strong, The New Strong's Expanded Exhaustive Concordance of the Bible (Thomas Nelson, 2010) 2263.

34. Merriam-Webster Online, s.v. "refrain," accessed November 20, 2017, https://www.merriam-webster.com/dictionary/refrain.

35. Rachaq—Hebrew meaning: James Strong, The New Strong's Expanded Exhaustive Concordance of the Bible (Thomas Nelson, 2010) 7368.

36. Merriam-Webster Online, s.v. "get," https://www.merriam-webster.com/dictionary/get.

37. Baqash—Hebrew meaning: James Strong, The New Strong's Expanded Exhaustive Concordance of the Bible (Thomas Nelson, 2010) 1245.

38. Merriam-Webster Online, s.v. "lose," accessed November 2, 2017, https://www.merriam-webster.com/dictionary/lose.

39. Abad—Hebrew meaning: James Strong, The New Strong's Expanded Exhaustive Concordance of the Bible (Thomas Nelson, 2010) 6.

40. Shamar—Hebrew meaning: James Strong, The New Strong's Expanded Exhaustive Concordance of the Bible (Thomas Nelson, 2010) 8104.

41. Merriam-Webster Online, s.v. "Definition of hedge about," accessed November 15, 2017, https://www.merriam-webster.com/dictionary/hedge_about.

42. Shalak—Hebrew meaning: James Strong, The New Strong's Expanded Exhaustive Concordance of the Bible (Thomas Nelson, 2010) 7993.

43. Merriam-Webster Online, s.v. "rend," https://www.merriam-webster.com/dictionary/ rend.

44. Qara—Hebrew meaning: James Strong, The New Strong's Expanded Exhaustive Concordance of the Bible (Thomas Nelson, 2010) 7167.

45. Merriam-Webster Online, LearnersDictionary.com, s.v. "sew,"
ttp://www.learnersdictionary.com/definition/sew.

46. Taphar—Hebrew meaning: James Strong, The New Strong's Expanded Exhaustive Concordance of the Bible (Thomas Nelson, 2010) 8609.

47. Chashah—Hebrew meaning: James Strong, The New Strong's Expanded Exhaustive Concordance of the Bible (Thomas Nelson, 2010) 2814.

48. Merriam-Webster Online, s.v. "silence," accessed November 24, 2017, https://www.merriam-webster.com/dictionary/silence.

49. Dabar—Hebrew meaning: James Strong, The New Strong's Expanded Exhaustive Concordance of the Bible (Thomas Nelson, 2010) 1696.

50. Ahab; aheb—Hebrew meaning: James Strong, The New Strong's Expanded Exhaustive Concordance of the Bible (Thomas Nelson, 2010) 157.

51. Sane—Hebrew meaning: James Strong, The New Strong's Expanded Exhaustive Concordance of the Bible (Thomas Nelson, 2010) 8130.

52. Milehamah—Hebrew meaning: James Strong, The New Strong's Expanded Exhaustive Concordance of the Bible (Thomas Nelson, 2010) 4421.

53. Shalom—Hebrew meaning: James Strong, The New Strong's Expanded Exhaustive Concordance of the Bible (Thomas Nelson, 2010) 7965.

MORE ABOUT THE AUTHOR

RHONDA ANDERSON is a Christian Author, a minister, prophetic intercessor; a teacher of the Bible; she also holds her degree in Theology.

Rhonda is the overseer of KIPM (Kingdom Investments Prayer Ministry). The ministry's primary focus is Intercessory Prayer with a mission to spread the Word God. Having a kingdom focus the ministry invests in reaching souls through several channels:

- Hosting teaching sessions/conferences
- Writing books
- Producing prayer products
- Teaching and preaching the gospel of the Kingdom of God

Her passion is ministering through her writing for the outreach of souls. Rhonda's scribing is a focus point of her daily walk and Christian lifestyle. She successfully published several books, including: Eyes of Understanding, Kingdom Intercession and an Intercessory Prayer Journal. One of her supporting scriptures for writing is Jeremiah (30:2); *"Thus speaketh the Lord God of Israel, saying, write thee all the words that I have spoken unto thee in a book."*

Rhonda strongly holds that God will use whosoever, to do whatsoever, to fulfill His purpose. She is the mother of two adult daughters; Keaonda & Alonda, one son-in-law Justin, and the happy grandmother of four grand-children: Alayjah, Jaliyah, Jaison and Eli.

Contact information: www.kipm.org/rhondaanderson